5./5

MAY 14

Is Online Addiction a Serious Problem?

Patricia D. Netzley

INCONTROVERSY

ReferencePoint
Press®

San Diego, CA

For more information, contact:
ReferencePoint Press, Inc.
PO Box 27779
San Diego, CA 92198
www.ReferencePointPress.com

LIBRARY OF CONGRESS CATALOGING-IN-PUBLICATION DATA

Netzley, Patricia D.
  Is online addiction a serious problem? / by Patricia D. Netzley.
    pages cm. -- (In controversy)
  Audience: Grade 9 to 12.
  Includes bibliographical references and index.
  ISBN-13: 978-1-60152-620-5 (hardback) -- ISBN-10: 1-60152-620-2 (hardback)
 1. Internet addiction--Popular works. I. Title.
  RC569.5.I54N48   2014
  616.85'84--dc23
                                                            2013029018

Contents

Foreword

In 2008, as the US economy and economies worldwide were falling into the worst recession since the Great Depression, most Americans had difficulty comprehending the complexity, magnitude, and scope of what was happening. As is often the case with a complex, controversial issue such as this historic global economic recession, looking at the problem as a whole can be overwhelming and often does not lead to understanding. One way to better comprehend such a large issue or event is to break it into smaller parts. The intricacies of global economic recession may be difficult to understand, but one can gain insight by instead beginning with an individual contributing factor, such as the real estate market. When examined through a narrower lens, complex issues become clearer and easier to evaluate.

This is the idea behind ReferencePoint Press's *In Controversy* series. The series examines the complex, controversial issues of the day by breaking them into smaller pieces. Rather than looking at the stem cell research debate as a whole, a title would examine an important aspect of the debate such as *Is Stem Cell Research Necessary?* or *Is Embryonic Stem Cell Research Ethical?* By studying the central issues of the debate individually, researchers gain a more solid and focused understanding of the topic as a whole.

Each book in the series provides a clear, insightful discussion of the issues, integrating facts and a variety of contrasting opinions for a solid, balanced perspective. Personal accounts and direct quotes from academic and professional experts, advocacy groups, politicians, and others enhance the narrative. Sidebars add depth to the discussion by expanding on important ideas and events. For quick reference, a list of key facts concludes every chapter. Source notes, an annotated organizations list, bibliography, and index provide student researchers with additional tools for papers and class discussion.

The *In Controversy* series also challenges students to think critically about issues, to improve their problem-solving skills, and to sharpen their ability to form educated opinions. As President Barack Obama stated in a March 2009 speech, success in the twenty-first century will not be measurable merely by students' ability to "fill in a bubble on a test but whether they possess 21st century skills like problem-solving and critical thinking and entrepreneurship and creativity." Those who possess these skills will have a strong foundation for whatever lies ahead.

No one can know for certain what sort of world awaits today's students. What we can assume, however, is that those who are inquisitive about a wide range of issues; open-minded to divergent views; aware of bias and opinion; and able to reason, reflect, and reconsider will be best prepared for the future. As the international development organization Oxfam notes, "Today's young people will grow up to be the citizens of the future: but what that future holds for them is uncertain. We can be quite confident, however, that they will be faced with decisions about a wide range of issues on which people have differing, contradictory views. If they are to develop as global citizens all young people should have the opportunity to engage with these controversial issues."

In Controversy helps today's students better prepare for tomorrow. An understanding of the complex issues that drive our world and the ability to think critically about them are essential components of contributing, competing, and succeeding in the twenty-first century.

Fun Activity or Uncontrollable Fixation?

The son of farmers in the rural village of Yujiatun, China, Jin Aibing worked hard to become one of the best students in his class. He had dreams of going to a top university, and after two tries he achieved a high score of 647 on China's college entrance exam. In 2004 he entered Jilin University in the northeastern city of Changchun. At first his studies there went well. But during his second year of college, he discovered online video gaming after friends showed him the game *World of Warcraft*. "I started playing that nonstop," he says. "Even in class, I would sit in the back and talk with my classmates about the game."[1] Soon he was skipping classes to frequent a nearby Internet café. He became fascinated with a Chinese online game called *Tianxia 3* (which means "The World 3"), and his study habits worsened. By his senior year he had failed six courses, and the university notified him that he would have to retake these courses to get his diploma. Instead, he opted to leave school.

Jin was too embarrassed to tell his family what he had done or even return to his rural village, because the people there had been so proud of him for getting into such a prestigious university. So he changed his cell phone number to cut ties to his past and went to live in the Internet café, where he could play video games all day long. In order to buy food there, he also started selling things he acquired by playing the game. He explains, "The Internet bar charged about 20 yuan ($3.22) per day with discounts. I started making a living by selling game currency for real money and made about 1,500 yuan a month."[2] When he was tired he slept on the café's sofas, and when he needed to shower he used facilities at his former university.

Eventually, other gamers began to notice that he never left the café, and a reporter did a story on him. This led both a university psychologist and a cousin to visit the café in an attempt to convince Jin to go home. After talking to his father on the phone at the psychologist's urging, Jin finally abandoned his life at the café and returned to his village. By this time it was March 2013, and he had lived in the café for four and a half years.

China's Response

Jin's story garnered a great deal of attention in China, where according to officials at least 24 million young people are addicted to online activities, particularly gaming. To address this problem, the government has taken measures to reduce teens' access to the Internet. For example, after several cases in the early 2000s in which bouts of continual online gaming led players to exhaust themselves to the point of physical harm, China banned teenagers from going into Internet cafés. It has also mandated that Chinese Internet gaming companies install a feature in their games requiring users to enter an ID card number that identifies which players are under eighteen. After three hours of play, the program tells the player to leave the game to engage in physical exercise, and if this instruction is not followed, points accrued during game play will disappear in stages until none remain.

But these measures have not solved the problem of excessive gaming among young adults in their twenties, like Jin. Consequently, in March 2013 Chinese authorities announced that government experts would be developing criteria for diagnosing people believed to be suffering from an Internet addiction in order to find and treat addicts still in the early stages of their addiction. Among the possible treatments is time spent in a military-style boot camp designed to cure the addiction.

Such camps first became popular in China in 2004 with the

Avid computer users, many of whom are young, fill every seat in an Internet café in China. Chinese authorities say that 24 million of the country's young people may be addicted to online activities, especially gaming.

establishment of the Internet Addiction Center in the city of Beijing. To date, this facility has treated more than three thousand teens and young adults for online addiction. It denies patients access to the Internet, cell phones, and other technological means of communication and forces them to follow a regimented daily schedule that includes military drills, therapy sessions, and time devoted to reading. The center also requires patients' parents to stay at the camp for their own version of treatment, based on the theory that parenting mistakes are to blame for children's addictions. Other centers, however, exclude parents, and some of these places have been involved in cases in which patients were beaten to death for failing to complete certain tasks or military drills.

Really an Addiction?

The parents of one such victim, a fifteen-year-old boy who attended the Qihang Salvation Training Camp in a rural area of southern China's Guangxi region, now say that fear-inducing stories in the media convinced them that their son was addicted to the Internet when in fact he was not. The boy's father, Deng Fei, states, "The Internet . . . wasn't really an addiction. It was his way out of the pressure of being a student."[3]

In the United States some experts would agree that the boy was never addicted to the Internet because they do not believe such an addiction is possible. Psychologist John M. Grohol is one such expert. He calls Internet addiction "one of those non-existent disorders that nonetheless actually has clinics devoted to its 'treatment,'" adding, "Internet addiction is a perfect example of a *fad disorder* brought about by its connection to the world's most popular communications and social network, the Internet."[4]

For more than a decade, Grohol has been speaking out against the tendency to lump the Internet in with addictions to drugs or alcohol. However, he acknowledges that his opinion might change if someone proves that the Internet really can be addictive. Indeed, many experts agree that there is inadequate research on this subject, and in May 2013 the American Psychiatric Association (APA) declared that because of this insufficiency, it would not include Internet addiction as a disorder in the newest edition of its *Diagnostic and Statistical Manual of Mental Disorders* (DSM). Used by clinicians and psychiatrists to diagnose psychiatric illnesses, this volume establishes what is or is not a treatable illness or disorder.

> "*Internet addiction is a perfect example of a fad disorder brought about by its connection to the world's most popular communications and social network, the Internet.*"[4]
>
> — Psychologist John M. Grohol.

Difficulty Getting Help

The APA's decision means that it will be costly for Americans who believe themselves to be suffering from online addiction to get treatment for it. This is because most insurance companies will not reimburse for the treatment of illnesses that are not listed in the DSM. But given that he thinks there is no such thing as a true Internet addiction, Grohol does not find this situation worrisome. In fact, he says, "Until there is stronger, more conclusive research in this area . . . you should shy away from anyone looking to treat this problem, since it is a problem that seems to exist more in some professionals' concept of *dysfunction* than in reality."[5]

Other mental health professionals, however, are extremely concerned about how the APA's decision will affect those who are truly suffering because of their Internet use. As psychiatrist Ronald Pies notes, such suffering does exist regardless of whether experts choose to label it the result of a mental disorder. Consequently, he says that although there is not enough data to conclude that Internet addiction is an illness, people who are suffering deserve some form of relief. He says, "Simply because someone does not fit criteria for *disease* (however defined), does not mean that he or she is unworthy of our professional aid and support."[6]

Experts disagree on how many people need this kind of support. Psychologist Kimberly S. Young, a leader in the treatment of Internet addicts, estimates that 5 to 10 percent of Internet users suffer from online addiction to varying degrees. But a study led by Dimitri A. Christakis, a professor of pediatrics at the University of Washington School of Public Health, reported in 2011 that among students at two US universities, excessive or addictive Internet use appeared in 4 percent of the population. While not a huge number, the researchers point out that this percentage does reflect a statistically significant group.

Addictive Activities

Many online activities can be considered addictive, especially gaming, gambling, shopping, viewing pornography, web surfing, and using social media sites like Twitter and Facebook. All types of people can develop an addiction to such activities. Psychiatrists Timothy Liu and Marc N. Potenza report that they have seen Problematic Internet Use (PIU) among young and old, men and women, and new and experienced computer users.

"The goal is not to eliminate technology from your life . . . [but to] limit your internet use and use the technological communication tools in a healthy way."[7]

— Lisa Haisha, a therapist who often writes about addictions to online social networking.

Experts in online addictions have also seen varying degrees of suffering related to PIU. Some addicts have such difficulty limiting their computer time that they cannot hold jobs and eventually drive their loved ones away. Others manage to keeps jobs and family relationships despite their addictions.

But although excessive Internet use can cause problems, the Internet has many positive aspects as well, and going online is difficult to avoid in modern society. According to Lisa Haisha, a therapist who often writes about addiction to online social networking, the Internet has been a wonderful thing, so "the goal is not to eliminate technology from your life, as that would be impossible in today's era," but to "limit your internet use and use the technological communication tools in a healthy way."[7] However, experts have yet to agree on just what constitutes a healthy use and on how best to address an unhealthy one.

Facts

- Tao Ran, the director of the Internet Addiction Center in Beijing, China, defines online addiction as six consecutive hours a day of Internet use for three months straight.

- As of June 2012, according to the China Internet Network Information Center, there were approximately 150 million Internet users in China under age nineteen, out of roughly 330 million users overall.

- The Internet use monitoring website Internet World Stats reports that nearly 80 percent of the population of North America uses the Internet.

- According to the Internet data collecting site StatCounter, as of July 2013 more than 90 percent of people searching the Internet used the Google search engine.

CHAPTER ONE

What Are the Origins of Online Addiction Concerns?

oncerns about online addictions began in the late 1970s and early 1980s, when the first opportunities arose for the general public to network with others via the Internet. This was the period when the first networked video games and the first online discussion groups appeared. As people discovered the attractions of interacting with others online, it became increasingly difficult for many to limit their computer time.

The first reference in print to the concept that such difficulties might represent a true addiction appeared in the 1979 book *An Introduction to Educational Computing* by British academic Nicholas Rushby. He also noted that some computer users seemed to suffer real withdrawal symptoms if they were kept from their computers. Another who noted this problem was British psychologist Margaret A. Shotton, who in the 1980s embarked on a study of psychological dependency on computer technology. Her work is considered pioneering in the field of computer addiction.

Shotton's study relied on questionnaires and in-person interviews completed by 106 people, most of them men in their twenties, who volunteered to work with her after having seen her newspaper advertisements seeking individuals who considered themselves to be computer dependent. Some of these individuals were computer programmers or others who used computers in their work, but many used computers only to play games during their off-work hours. Consequently, Shotton's research primarily concerns gaming addictions.

In reporting on Shotton's work, some psychologists criticized her for the way in which she chose and surveyed her subjects. By using people who had sought her out and had already identified themselves as computer dependent, these critics argued, Shotton might have slanted her work so that it featured only computer-dependent users who were willing to admit they had a problem. This is known as sampling bias. In addition, critics noted, relying on test subjects to provide all information regarding their computer use could lead to errors arising from participants misestimating the amount of time they spent playing video games and/or giving false impressions regarding how their behavior was affecting their loved ones.

Nonetheless, Shotton drew conclusions from her work that many mental health experts consider to be valid. In her 1989 book *Computer Addiction? A Study of Computer Dependency*, she reported that computers could seem to provide more companionship and partnership than a pet. She also noted that many of her subjects had lacked parental love and warmth during their childhoods, and she believed that they were drawn to computers in large part to compensate for this lack. However, Shotton also concluded that while Internet addiction exists, it is not a clinical pathology (that is, not a mental disease), nor does it pose a threat to computer users. In fact, in 1991 she suggested that any harm from excessive Internet use was more than outweighed by its benefits, among them the Internet's ability to provide a safe haven for people feeling overwhelmed by problems in their daily life.

Focusing on Women

Even though Shotton's study primarily involved men, she believed that women were as much at risk for computer addiction as men. Nonetheless, many people interpreted her findings as meaning that far more men than women became dependent on comput-

The DSM

When the APA published the first edition of the *Diagnostic and Statistical Manual of Mental Disorders* (DSM-I) in 1952, it was a thin, spiral-bound volume that listed only 106 mental disorders. At the time, it was intended merely as a guide to help identify these disorders. But this changed in 1980 with the publication of the third edition, DSM-III, a 494-page work that listed 265 disorders. This edition broke new ground by establishing explicit diagnostic criteria for what constituted valid mental disorders and creating a standard language for discussing such disorders.

A revised edition of the DSM-III appeared in 1987, a fourth edition in 1994, a revised fourth edition in 2000, and a fifth edition in 2013. Although the publication of each new edition brought concerns that the definition of a mental disorder was becoming too broad, there was an increase in listed disorders from one volume to the next. The DSM-IV had 297, the revised DSM-IV 374. Then criticism over the burgeoning list of disorders led the APA to alter its classification system prior to publishing the DSM-V in 2013 so that certain disorders became subcategories of others. Nonetheless, this edition is 992 pages long. It does not include Internet addiction as a disorder or as a subcategory, although its possible inclusion was the subject of debate before publication.

ers. As a result, the media began to stereotype computer addicts as lonely, unhappy young men. This image persisted until psychologist Kimberly S. Young showed that just as many women as men suffered from computer addiction, sometimes with extreme consequences. Young founded the Center for Internet Addiction, a prominent research and treatment center, in 1995.

The initial goal of Young's research was to find out whether Internet addiction was real. In writing years later about how she came to embark on a two-year study of Internet-related behaviors in 1994, she said, "After a friend called me to tell me of her divorce because her husband became addicted to AOL chat rooms, it made me wonder if others could get addicted to the Internet in the same way as people become addicted to drugs, alcohol, gambling, food, and sex."[8]

When she began her studies, Young attracted subjects for her research by placing ads in newspapers and on college campuses, posting in online support groups, and searching for comments on websites that referenced Internet addiction. Eventually, she was able to recruit for her case studies 396 individuals who identified themselves as being dependent on the Internet.

Unlike Shotton, however, Young received responses to her ads and posts from 20 percent more women than men. She later said, "This result shows a significant discrepancy from the stereotypic profile of an 'Internet addict' as a young, computer-savvy male and is counter to previous research that has suggested males predominantly utilize and feel comfortable with information technologies."[9] But Young added that this does not necessarily mean there are more female computer addicts than male ones; it just means that women might be more comfortable discussing the topic.

Breaking a Stereotype

Because women had been neglected in discussions of computer addiction, Young chose to do more in-depth research on one of the women in her study, a forty-three-year-old housewife whose life had fallen apart because of her online activities. This case, Young said, showed "that a non-technologically oriented woman with a reportedly content home life and no prior addiction or psychiatric history abused the Internet which resulted in significant impairment to her family life."[10] Young spent six months interviewing the woman, and in 1996 the psychologist presented her work in a paper titled "Psychology of Computer Use"—the first case study related to Internet addiction ever published.

In presenting the case, Young reported that although the

woman had initially been afraid to use a computer when she got her first one, she had a relatively easy time figuring out how to use it. However, she only used it to go online, and within three months of discovering Internet chat rooms that allowed her to socialize with other users in real time, she was spending fifty to sixty hours a week on her computer. The woman told Young that when she developed a sense of community while participating in certain chat rooms, she usually stayed online far longer than intended. Her chat sessions could last as long as fourteen hours, sometimes going through the night, and the woman also obsessively checked her e-mail off and on all day long.

As a result, Young said of the woman, "she eventually felt depressed, anxious, and irritable whenever she was not in front of her computer. In an effort to avoid what she referred to as 'withdrawal from the Internet,' she engaged in activities to stay on-line as long as she could."[11] This meant canceling appointments, avoiding offline friends, largely ignoring her husband and two daughters, abandoning social activities like her bridge club, and failing to perform household chores. She also refused her husband's request that she get treatment for her addiction, and within one year of her getting a computer, he had left her, and her daughters wanted nothing to do with her. Young added that after these losses, the woman realized that she was suffering from an addiction that was similar to alcoholism and was able to reduce her time online without any help from others, although she could not end it completely.

Identifying a Problem

In addition to bringing more attention to the plight of female computer addicts, Young's studies of such addicts as a whole found marked similarities between the behavior exhibited by dependent computer users and the behavior of people addicted to alcohol and drugs. Therefore, Young and her supporters felt that she had proved that Internet addiction was a real affliction. Young also urged more mental health professionals to study Internet addiction.

In a paper that Young presented to the APA in August 1996, she said that, on the basis of her findings, "future research should develop treatment protocols and conduct outcome studies for ef-

fective management of . . . symptoms." She added that "future research should focus on the prevalence, incidence, and the role of this type of behavior in other established addictions (e.g., other substance dependencies or pathological gambling) or psychiatric disorders (e.g., depression, bipolar disorder, obsessive-compulsive disorder, attention deficit disorder)."[12] To Young, research into on-line addictions could benefit sufferers of other addictions.

Young's paper on Internet addiction also offered criteria by which Internet addiction could be diagnosed, something that no one had ever attempted to provide before. This diagnostic tool was in the form of a series of questions, the Internet Addiction Diagnostic Questionnaire, that individuals who believed themselves to be suffering from Internet addiction could answer to determine whether they did indeed have a problem. In its original version, this test asked eight questions, the answers to which could only be either *yes* or *no*. According to Young, answering *yes* to five or more

Early research on Internet dependence focused mostly on males. Experts today know that females are just as likely to experience online addictions as males.

of these questions indicated that the person had an online addiction. These questions were:

1. Do you feel preoccupied with the Internet (think about previous online activity or anticipate next online session)?
2. Do you feel the need to use the Internet with increasing amounts of time in order to achieve satisfaction?
3. Have you repeatedly made unsuccessful efforts to control, cut back, or stop Internet use?
4. Do you feel restless, moody, depressed, or irritable when attempting to cut down or stop Internet use?
5. Do you stay online longer than originally intended?
6. Have you jeopardized or risked the loss of significant relationship, job, educational or career opportunity because of the Internet?
7. Have you lied to family members, therapists, or others to conceal the extent of involvement with the Internet?
8. Do you use the Internet as a way of escaping from problems or of relieving a dysphoric mood (e.g., feelings of helplessness, guilt, anxiety, depression)?[13]

As Young gathered more information about online addiction, however, she altered her test. The current version has twenty questions, to which the answer choices are *rarely, occasionally, frequently, often, always,* or *does not apply.* Among these questions are "How often do you neglect household chores to spend more time on-line?," "How often do others in your life complain to you about the amount of time you spend on-line?," "How often do your grades or school work suffer because of the amount of time you spend on-line?," and "How often do you become defensive or secretive when anyone asks you what you do on-line?"[14]

Real Diagnostics or Bad Science?

Young's questionnaire quickly became popular—ironically, largely because it was posted on the Internet—and it remains in use today. But the questionnaire is not without its critics. For example, Virginia Heffernan, author of the book *Magic and Loss: The Pleasures of the Internet,* says that the test ignores the fact that the Internet is

simply more entertaining than doing or thinking about activities like chores and schoolwork. She explains:

> In the hierarchy of the test, any real-world task or interaction, no matter how mundane or tedious, is more important—and, worse, ought to be more fulfilling—than online fantasy, research or social life. "Do you neglect household chores to use the Internet?" one question asks, and undone laundry is later cited as a warning sign. "How often do you block out disturbing thoughts about your life with soothing thoughts of the Internet?" goes another question. Can this really be science?[15]

Others ridiculed the very notion that excessive Internet use could be considered a mental disorder, especially after Young published the first book on Internet addiction, *Caught in the Net*, in 1998. Later she wrote, "After *Caught in the Net* was published,

Some studies suggest that people addicted to drugs such as cocaine (pictured) and people with online addictions exhibit similar behaviors. The steps required for diagnosing and treating online addiction are less developed than for other addictions.

many journalists and scholars did not believe that people could become addicted to the Internet. At that point, many laughed and scoffed at the idea. How could a tool so useful for information and communication be considered addictive?"[16]

Goldberg's Parody

One of the first people to ridicule the concept of online addictions, however, did so as part of a joke. This was New York psychiatrist Ivan Goldberg, who in the 1980s had established an online forum for psychiatrists that featured bulletin boards where people could form groups and post messages to fellow members. In 1995 Goldberg decided to post a parody on the board that would poke fun at the APA's *Diagnostic and Statistical Manual of Mental Disorders* (DSM).

As part of this joke, he created a mental disorder he called Internet addiction disorder (IAD), thereby becoming the first person to use this term. Goldberg also came up with what he called "the official criteria for the diagnosis of IAD," which included not only the behaviors that researchers like Young had noted but also the physical symptoms of "voluntary or involuntary typing of the fingers" and "psychomotor agitation."[17] When Goldberg posted his parody online, he thought his fellow psychiatrists would take it as the joke he intended it to be. Instead, some of them started contacting him about their own online addictions.

Goldberg then took the joke one step further, setting up a bogus online support group, the Internet Addiction Support Group, and announcing it in a post under the name E. Guy Coffee. But again people took his work seriously. In fact, hundreds of people joined the group in order to share stories of their addictions, a development that Goldberg found alarming. He later said that having a support group for Internet addicts "makes as much sense as having a support group for coughers." His real term for excessive Internet use, he says, is "pathological Internet-use disorder," explaining, "To medicalize every behavior by putting it into psychiatric nomenclature is ridiculous."[18]

"To medicalize every behavior by putting it into psychiatric nomenclature is ridiculous."[18]

— New York psychiatrist Ivan Goldberg.

Hearing from Sufferers

But Goldberg's critics note that he is a specialist in bipolar disorder, not addiction, and therefore has not heard as many stories of Internet addiction as the experts in this field have. It is these stories that have spurred people like Young to continue pushing for the inclusion of Internet addiction in the DSM.

Young's book *Caught in the Net* was intended to reach out to sufferers, reassure them that they had a real disorder, and offer them hope that they could get help for their problem. After its publication, Young said, "Letters and email from across the globe poured in. I heard from parents, spouses, and addicts themselves struggling to deal with an addiction that they could not understand. Yet, after reading *Caught in the Net*, they found validation and understanding [for] a disorder that they knew they were experiencing but had not been recognized by many professionals when they tried to seek help."[19]

Young also heard from people who agreed with her position that more attention needed to be paid to the prevention of online addiction. In *Caught in the Net*, she wrote, "We're assured that [the Internet] will only improve and enrich our lives. It has the capability. But it also has an addictive potential with harmful consequences that, left undetected and unchecked, could silently run rampant in our schools, our universities, our offices, our libraries, and our homes."[20]

> "We're assured that [the Internet] will only improve and enrich our lives. It has the capability. But it also has an addictive potential with harmful consequences that, left undetected and unchecked, could silently run rampant in our schools, our universities, our offices, our libraries, and our homes."[20]
>
> — Psychologist Kimberly S. Young.

Concerns Increase

As Internet use grew during the 2000s, concerns about Internet addiction grew as well. Most of the research inspired by this concern was in Asia, particularly South Korea. In the mid-2010s, South Korea declared Internet addiction a major health problem, estimating that more than 200,000 South Koreans under the age of nineteen required treatment for their addiction and that 1.2 million young adults were at risk for becoming addicted.

Some experts believe that the problem of Internet addiction is just as serious in the United States but is not as easily detectable. This is because of the difference in how the Internet is accessed. In Asia, Internet cafés are the most common place to be while going online, whereas in the United States the Internet is most often accessed from home. Moreover, perhaps because of the more private nature of accessing the Internet in the United States, according to psychiatrist Jerald J. Block, "attempts to measure the phenomenon [of Internet addiction] are clouded by shame, denial, and minimi-

Deadly Consequences

Sometimes an online addiction can have deadly consequences. There have been at least ten documented cases of people dying from blood clots, caused by sitting in front of a computer too long, that migrated to the heart or lungs. In 2012, for example, officials in Taiwan attributed two deaths to marathon sessions of online gaming. In one, a young man died slumped in a chair, his hands still on the keyboard, after playing for twenty-three hours straight. In another, an eighteen-year-old collapsed in a private room of an Internet café and subsequently died at a local hospital after playing an online game for two days straight without eating or drinking. There have also been cases in the United States and elsewhere of doctors having to amputate a player's leg because of a clot caused by a marathon gaming session. Online addictions can physically harm an addict's loved ones as well. This was the case with the three-year-old daughter of Rebecca Colleen Christie of Las Cruces, New Mexico. In 2011 Christie, age twenty-eight, was convicted of murder after her addiction to playing *World of Warcraft* led her to neglect her little girl to the point of severe malnutrition and dehydration—and death.

zation." He reports that roughly 86 percent of Internet addiction cases are accompanied by a diagnosis of some other kind of mental disorder. Therefore, he says, "unless the therapist is specifically looking for Internet addiction, it is unlikely to be detected. In Asia, however, therapists are taught to screen for it."[21]

Block is one of the foremost American experts on video game addiction, and in 2008 he wrote an article arguing for the inclusion of Internet addiction in the DSM. But he also suggested that not much would be gained by providing more treatment for Internet addiction. He said, "Unfortunately, Internet addiction is resistant to treatment, entails significant risks, and has high relapse rates."[22] Other experts have noted that it is difficult to combat Internet addiction because the best way to do this would be for the sufferer to stop using the Internet altogether. Such abstinence is not possible for many people, particularly now that going online to search for information, surf websites, shop, play games, socialize, and check e-mail has become such an integral part of modern life.

> *"Unfortunately, Internet addiction is resistant to treatment, entails significant risks, and has high relapse rates."*[22]
>
> — Psychiatrist Jerald J. Block.

Treatment Centers

Nonetheless, in the mid- to late 1990s a few mental health professionals in the United States began to establish treatment centers for Internet addicts. One of the most prominent experts during this period was Maressa Orzack, who became interested in computer addiction after she found herself excessively playing a computer solitaire card game. At the time, she was treating patients for gambling addictions and substance abuse problems; she recognized her own obsessive card playing as being similar to the impulse control problems her patients were exhibiting. This led her to open a clinic for Internet addicts in 1996 at McLean Hospital, a psychiatric hospital in Massachusetts affiliated with Harvard University. At the Computer Addiction Study Center, she initially saw no more than two patients a week, but by 2006 she was seeing dozens of patients a week. Much of this increase was undoubtedly due to the explosive growth of the Internet during this period, since experts estimate that between March 2000 and

March 2013, the number of Internet users worldwide grew from 304 million to more than 2.5 billion.

With more users came more US treatment centers for Internet addicts. Among the most prominent are the Center for Internet and Technology Addiction in West Hartford, Connecticut; the Illinois Institute for Addiction Recovery at Proctor Hospital in Peoria, Illinois; and the reSTART Internet Addiction Recovery Program in Fall City, Washington. Founded in 2009, reSTART was the first inpatient residential care center to open in the United States. However, this facility can only treat six patients at a time, and similar facilities are few and also have limited space. This is a matter of great concern for experts who believe that far more people are suffering from an online addiction than are able to receive help for it.

Facts

- A national study conducted by a team from Stanford University's School of Medicine estimated that nearly one in eight Americans suffers from at least one sign of problematic Internet use.

- According to the International Telecommunication Union, a United Nations agency specializing in information and communication technologies, in March 2013 the number of Internet users worldwide represented 38.8 percent of the global population.

- South Korea has more than 140 Internet addiction treatment centers.

- According to the online site Internet World Stats, between 2000 and 2009 the rate of increase in the number of Internet users in Africa and the Middle East exceeded 1,300 percent.

Are Online Addictions Real Addictions?

I n February 2013 researchers at Swansea University in the United Kingdom and Milan University in Italy released the results of a joint study that showed that heavy Internet users prevented from accessing the Internet experience psychological withdrawal symptoms similar to those experienced by drug users. The researchers began the study by questioning sixty volunteers on their amount of computer use in order to determine which ones might be considered addicted to the Internet. These test subjects, whose average age was twenty-five, were then asked to spend fifteen minutes on the Internet—doing whatever activities they chose. Afterward they were instructed not to use the Internet. During this period, researchers evaluated the test subjects' mood changes and found that the subjects demonstrated an increase in anxiety, irritation, and other negative emotions as more time passed following their Internet session. Phil Reed, one of the Swansea researchers, reports, "When these people come off-line, they suffer increased negative mood—just like people coming off illegal drugs like Ecstasy."[23]

Some experts take the comparison between Internet use and drug use one step further, believing that both elicit physical

> "When these people come off-line, they suffer increased negative mood— just like people coming off illegal drugs like Ecstasy."[23]
>
> — Addiction researcher Phil Reed.

Surfing Depression

Many people who suffer from Internet addiction are also suffering from clinical depression. Most experts in the field of addiction believe that the two disorders go hand in hand because the Internet can be used to stave off depression. That is, the depression exists before the problematic Internet use, and the addict is using the Internet to cope with depression. But recent research suggests that in some cases, surfing the web can actually cause depression where none existed before. For example, in 2010 researchers at the University of Notre Dame in Fremantle, Australia, and Guangzhou University in China, studied a group of more than one thousand Chinese high school students who reported having no symptoms of depression at the start of the study. Nine months later 8 percent of the students had developed depression, with those who had become moderate to heavy users of the Internet during the course of the study being two and a half times more likely to be among the depressed.

changes in the brain. Researchers have long known that regular use of a drug can cause such changes as a result of the biochemical and structural adaptations that the body makes in response to the drug. Once access to the drug is withdrawn, it can take the central nervous system days or weeks to return to normal. A few studies suggest that Internet addiction might also cause this kind of response. Recent research in China, for example, suggests that over time, the brains of heavy Internet users experience a reduction in volume and a decrease in white matter, a tissue in the brain that contains nerve fiber. The longer the addiction persists, the greater these alterations are.

In other studies, brain scans of heavy Internet users have shown changes in the parts of the brain associated with attention control, executive control (the mechanism that allows for goal-directed action), and emotion processing. However, experts disagree as to whether heavy Internet use was the cause of these changes. As psychologist Alice G. Walton notes, "It's not clear whether people became addicted to the Internet first and brain changes then followed, or whether the brain was already wired differently, predisposing the young brains to addiction."[24]

Still other studies suggest that the brains of Internet addicts might be different in regard to dopamine, a neurotransmitter and neurohormone produced in several areas of the brain. Dopamine is involved in cognition, attention, memory, motivation, sleep, and mood, among other functions, but is perhaps best known for its connection to pleasure. Whenever a person does something that causes pleasure, the level of dopamine in the brain rises. Some researchers believe that certain brains develop a need for this higher level, producing cravings or addictions in order to encourage a repeat of the pleasurable experience.

Kristen Lindquist, professor of psychology at the University of North Carolina–Chapel Hill, is among those who believe that dopamine drives addiction. She says that people addicted to social media, for example, get a jolt of dopamine whenever someone responds positively to their tweet or Facebook status, and "as with cocaine addicts, over time you need more and more of that substance to get that feeling."[25]

"The popular myth would suggest everything we like could be addictive: reading books, scratching an itch, building model steamships out of matchsticks, whatever floats your boat."[27]

— Neuropsychologist Vaughan Bell.

Pseudoscience

Others ridicule the notion that engaging in an Internet activity like spending time on Facebook elicits a physical response similar to the ones seen in drug users. Some of these people argue that the research suggesting the existence of a physical response is flawed. Others insist that the appearance of a physical response in someone who uses the Internet heavily is a coincidence. Still others say that even if Internet use does change human bodies in some way, these changes do not drive someone to crave the Internet the way a drug addict craves drugs.

Vaughan Bell, a clinical and neuropsychologist at the University of Antioquia in Colombia and King's College London, is among those who do not believe that a physical response to spending time online causes people to increase their use of the Internet. Specifically, he calls the idea that dopamine equals addiction "a vacuous piece of pseudo-neuroscience" and a "fallacy often touted by mental health professionals as a substantive explanation when it is nothing of the sort." Just because dopamine levels change during pleasurable activities, Bell says, does not mean dopamine makes people engage in that activity. He explains:

> We know that dopamine is involved in pleasure and desire, and that drug addiction causes long-term changes to the dopamine system that likely weaken our impulse control and draw our attention to reminders of drugs and drug-taking. There are subtle but important differences between these two statements, though. The former refers to an instant reaction to any pleasurable activity, while the latter indicates a possibly permanent change in how the brain reacts to the world owing to the use of substances which artificially alter it.[26]

Bell also points out that dopamine rises when people engage in any enjoyable activities, most of which do not lead to addiction. Therefore, he says,

> there's no direct one-to-one relationship between dopamine and addiction, and knowing that this particular brain chemical is released during an activity predicts nothing about how problematic the activity might be. As the dopamine system starts working when we encounter anything pleasurable, the popular myth would suggest everything we like could be addictive: reading books, scratching an itch, building model steamships out of matchsticks, whatever floats your boat.[27]

A Matter of Choice?

Other experts suggest that when it comes to pleasurable activities, what looks like an addiction might just be a temporary passion that will revert to a more normal level of activity with time. But

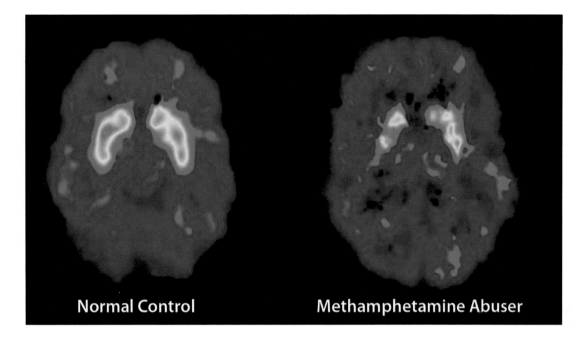

Normal Control　　　　**Methamphetamine Abuser**

even if this level of activity remains intense, such experts say, it is simply because the individual engaging in the activity enjoys it to the exclusion of other, less appealing activities. In other words, the amount of time that people spend on the Internet—even if that amount of time is excessive—is a matter of choice.

Gene Heyman, a research psychologist at McLean Hospital and a lecturer at Harvard University, is among those who believe that Internet use is always the result of a choice rather than a compulsion. In fact, he believes that addictions to drugs, tobacco, and alcohol are also a matter of choice. He bases his argument on national surveys of addicts' ability to quit an addiction. Heyman reports that the quit rate was roughly 75 percent, which means that most of the addicts surveyed were actually ex-addicts. The majority had stopped using drugs at clinically significant levels by the time they were thirty to thirty-five years old.

This suggests that as addicts age, most stop being addicts. But how do they manage to stop? Heyman reports that surveys show that more than 70 percent did so on their own, without seeking professional help, and typically their success was preceded by concerns about their finances, family relationships, job, or health.

Dopamine plays a crucial role in the brain's reward and pleasure pathways; it is an important factor in drug addiction and may also be involved in online addiction. A comparison of a normal brain and the brain of a methamphetamine addict reveals more dopamine transporters (bright areas) in the nonuser than the addict. Meth decreases the number of dopamine transporters, causing users to need more and more of the drug to get the same effect.

Heyman says, "In other words, the usual factors that influence everyday decisions helped addicts quit drugs." He adds, however, that the choices that addicts make are not about being an addict but about behaving or not behaving in certain ways. He explains, "I do not mean to say that someone chooses to be an addict. Rather, they choose to have just one more drink or quit tomorrow. A long enough series of one-more-times makes an addict. Addicts tend to quit when the 'hassles' of maintaining their habit become too great (sometimes called 'hitting bottom')."[28]

> "Addicts tend to quit when the 'hassles' of maintaining their habit become too great (sometimes called 'hitting bottom')."[28]
>
> — Psychologist Gene Heyman.

Many people disagree with Heyman that all addiction is a choice. But many agree with him in regard to addictive behaviors as opposed to addictive substances. In fact, Sara Kiesler, a professor of computer science and human-computer interaction at Carnegie Mellon University, recently conducted a study in which a majority of heavy Internet users were able to significantly reduce their computer use over a period of one year simply by having the will to do so. Consequently, she says that calling excessive Internet use an addiction belittles physiological addictions like those to drugs and cigarettes, which she calls genuinely serious illnesses.

Mood Changes

Kiesler also thinks that all Internet use, even excessive use, is harmless. She says, "I think using the Internet in certain ways can be quite absorbing, but I don't know that it's any different from an addiction to playing the violin and bowling. There is absolutely no evidence that spending time online, exchanging e-mail with family and friends, is the least bit harmful. We know that people who are depressed or anxious are likely to go online for escape and that doing so helps them."[29]

Indeed, many psychologists note that the Internet can draw people seeking to change their mood, much the way drug addicts seek out drugs largely to change their mood. In both cases the seeker is typically trying to eliminate depression and anxiety. These emotions are also associated with withdrawal from both activities, a commonality that has led some experts to say that both emotions are the key to determining whether or why Internet use might be genuinely addictive. Consequently, several recent studies have looked at what happens to Internet users who are forced to go through withdrawal.

In one such study reported in April 2013, researchers at the University of Winchester in the United Kingdom asked twenty volunteers who had diagnosed themselves as being addicted to Internet social networking to stop using these services for four weeks. Specifically, ten claimed to be addicted to Facebook and ten to Twitter, saying they accessed the Internet several times a day by computer or by smartphone. During the first week of the study, many of the participants suffered serious distress and seemed incapable of communicating by other means. "I haven't communicated with my family all week," one Facebook addict complained, and another reported, "I've felt alone and cut off from the world."[30]

Over the course of the study, some of the participants showed an ability to reconnect with the world and engage in activities they had abandoned while hooked on the Internet, such as doing chores and spending time with loved ones. But those who had been hooked on Twitter were much more able to do these things than the Facebook addicts. The difference, researchers say, might be in the ways the two sites are used. Twitter simply involves sending and reading brief messages, whereas Facebook involves multiple activities, like sharing pictures, engaging in conversations, and playing games, making it more engaging and more social.

"There is absolutely no evidence that spending time online, exchanging e-mail with family and friends, is the least bit harmful."[29]

— Sara Kiesler, a professor of computer science and human-computer interaction at Carnegie Mellon University.

Addictive Personalities

The researchers also compared the experiences of their Twitter and Facebook addicts with another group of twenty people who were uninterested in using Facebook or Twitter. Ten of these people had once tried Twitter and Facebook but let their accounts fall inactive. The other ten had never used any form of social networking. Both groups were asked to tweet and update their Facebook status as much as possible over a period of four weeks. At the end of the

study period, some found these activities pleasurable. One said, "I thought I would find using Facebook every day dull and pointless, but I'm finding that I'm quite enjoying it. I'm actually seeing my friends more now."[31] However, none had become addicted to the activities.

The fact that being forced to use the Internet excessively does not necessarily lead to addictive behaviors suggests that perhaps only certain types of people become Internet addicts. Indeed, in the late 1980s many experts began to believe in the existence of an addictive personality—a set of personality traits that leads people to be more prone to addiction. These traits include being impulsive, nonconformist, and emotionally insecure.

Craig Nakken, who helped establish the popular notion of an addictive personality through the 1988 publication of his book *The Addictive Personality*, has suggested that another common trait among all addicts is the desire to become lost in a trancelike state.

He explains, "The trance allows addicts to detach from the pain, guilt, and shame they feel, making it extremely attractive. The addict becomes increasingly skillful at living in the trance and using it to cover painful feelings. In the process, he or she gets a sense of power and control, but also becomes dependent on the trance, which is part of the addictive process."[32]

Psychological Problems

Today the idea that there is a true addictive personality is a matter of great disagreement among experts in the field of addiction. However, many have noted that addicts share certain individual personality traits, and a desire to escape painful feelings and the problems of daily life is one of them. The Internet can provide a welcome distraction for troubled people, and some of these individuals are able to find resources online, including friends, that help them cope better with their difficulties.

But some researchers have suggested that deeper, less easily solved problems are behind Internet addiction. Specifically, they see a connection between Internet addiction and psychiatric disorders. In one study in 2006, researchers at the Yongin Mental Hospital in South Korea used the Internet Addiction Scale established by American psychologist Kimberly S. Young to identify twelve adolescents with Internet addiction. Through further study, they determined that five of these individuals had preexisting depressive disorders. The researchers therefore theorized that Internet addiction is a symptom of depressive disorders, at least in adolescents.

A 2008 German study of thirty Internet addicts had similar results, finding that twenty-seven of the addicts had previously been diagnosed with a psychiatric disorder. In comparison, only seven of a group of thirty-one people who were not addicted to the Internet had been previously diagnosed with a psychiatric disorder. These researchers concluded that their results cast doubt on whether Internet addiction can exist independently from a psychiatric disorder.

Do Labels Matter?

Whether heavy use of the Internet should be classified as a disease or merely a symptom of a disease does not concern most people who believe they are suffering from Internet addiction. They just want help for what ails them. But experts say that the label matters a great deal, not only in terms of what courses of treatment might be best but in regard to how the label affects the psychology of the sufferer.

For example, Bell reports that according to studies in Canada, "if we replace a common name for an illness with a medical term—

Genes for Addiction

Studies have long shown that 50 to 60 percent of substance addiction is due to genetic factors, which is perhaps why the children of people addicted to drugs or alcohol are eight times more likely to develop a similar addiction themselves. Now researchers are beginning to examine whether behavioral addictions could also have a genetic component. In August 2012 researchers from the University of Bonn and the Central Institute of Mental Health in Mannheim, both in Germany, announced evidence that suggests this might be the case with Internet addiction. As reported in the September 2012 issue of the *Journal of Addiction Medicine*, the study compared the genetic makeup of two groups: the first group consisted of problematic Internet users and the second, known as a control group, consisted of people who did not have that problem. The study found that most people in the first group carried a genetic variation that studies of nicotine addicts have shown promotes addictive behavior. Researchers involved in the nicotine studies concluded that this variation changes the genetic makeup for a receptor tied to the brain's reward system, and the German researchers have suggested that the same effect might be involved in Internet addiction.

pharyngitis for *sore throat*, e.g.—people tend to perceive the illness as being more serious."[33] He also reports that when people are told that they have a mental disorder and this diagnosis is described solely in biological or clinical terms, sufferers come away feeling as though they have no control over their bodies and therefore no control over their actions, either. Consequently, Bell argues that talking about excessive Internet use as though it were a disease encourages people to view themselves as slaves to Internet-damaged brains and gives them an excuse to keep on engaging in behavior that does them no good.

New York psychologist Todd Essig argued against the inclusion of *Internet addiction* in the DSM-V for reasons similar to those cited by Bell. He believes that excessive use of the Internet, like many other excessive behaviors (such as hoarding), can be controlled. But once they are labeled as mental disorders, the individuals who suffer from them might instead view themselves as suffering from a disorder over which they have no control. He explains, "Making bad choices, developing destructive habits, and attempting solutions to problems in living that then become serious problems themselves will all become less important as the locus of responsibility shifts from the person doing something to the something being done."[34]

Labeling a behavior a disease is also a way to suggest that a particular activity is bad and should therefore be avoided at all costs. As Virginia Heffernan notes, "Virtually all non-work activities have, at one time or another, been represented as craven and diseased."[35] In the eighteenth century, for example, women were repeatedly told that reading was bad for them because it would expose them to unhealthy ideas that would eventually corrupt the body as well as the mind. Another warning from this period led to the idea of addiction. In cautioning against the dangers of alcohol as part of a temperance campaign, eighteenth-century physician Benjamin Rush called drinking a disease of the will, and by the nineteenth century, people believed that weak wills were more susceptible to alcoholism. This suggested that only the inferior drank, and gradually the concept of weak wills became weak—or diseased—minds.

Social Activities

But some point out that labeling a behavior excessive is a matter of judgment. What is too much to one person is just right to another. And critics of the label *Internet addiction* argue that people are too quick today to label excessive Internet use a problem. Heffernan, for example, argues that spending a lot of time on the Internet is not necessarily bad. She insists that even if chores are being missed or sleep being lost, if a student is getting good grades then there's no reason to argue that that student should be spending more time reading classic literature or playing chess.

Psychologist John M. Grohol shares the view that Internet use should not be judged so harshly. He says:

> Would we ever characterize any time spent in the real world with friends as "addicting?" Of course not. Teenagers talk on the phone for hours on end, with people they see every day! Do we say they are addicted to the telephone? Of course not. People lose hours at a time, immersed in a book, ignoring friends and family, and often not even picking up the phone when it rings. Do we say they are addicted to the book? Of course not.[36]

Nonetheless, there are ample stories of people who have trouble controlling their use of the Internet, and many reports of individuals whose lives have been ruined by their online excesses. Hours have slipped away, families have broken up, and fortunes, jobs, and opportunities have been lost to the allures of the Internet. In the face of such experiences, it is difficult for those who treat Internet addicts to see the experiences of their patients as anything but an addiction.

Facts

- Studies at universities in South Korea in 2011 and China in 2012 found that the brains of people suffering from Internet addiction had reduced dopamine receptors and impaired dopamine function.

- Addictions to a behavior are generally known as process addictions, and addictions to drugs, tobacco, or alcohol are called substance addictions.

- In 2010 researchers in China proposed that a diagnosis of Internet addiction only be made if symptoms had been ongoing for at least three months and involved at least six hours per day of nonessential Internet use. A 2011 study in Connecticut found that among high school students, problematic Internet use was most common among Asians and Hispanics and more common among boys than girls.

- According to studies in Asia, young people who suffer from Internet addiction are also more likely to suffer from depression, impulsive behavior, and social phobias.

CHAPTER THREE

Are Addictions to Online Shopping and Social Networking Serious Problems?

Americans spend more time on social networking sites than any other online activity. This is the finding of a 2013 survey by the consumer and business credit reporting company Experian. The survey found that of all the minutes Americans spend online, sixteen minutes of every online hour is spent on social networking sites. Entertainment websites are next, at nine minutes per online hour, followed by online shopping, at five minutes per online hour.

Online social networking and online shopping appeal to people for many different reasons. One thing they have in common is that they can be addictive. Many people have reported difficulty limiting the time and money they spend on these activities.

Addictions to social networking and online shopping can start at a young age—according to researchers, typically in the teens or early twenties. Some cases begin even earlier. In a March 2013 online post titled "I Was a Preteen eBay Addict," blogger Elizabeth M. Beck confesses to having become addicted to the auction and shopping website when she was in the seventh grade. This addiction began shortly after her mother gave her an American Express credit card. Provided for the first time with the means to buy things online, Beck soon found herself bidding on items that she could not afford. She says, "I spent $80 on South Park bumper stickers and back-issues of *Seventeen* from the late 90s."[37]

Then she realized there was no way for her to get eighty dollars to repay her mother for what she had spent. She says, "In a panic, I submitted requests for all of my won auctions to rescind my winnership. . . . Needless to say, eBay totally banned my account."[38] This meant that Beck could not participate in any more auctions. But when her address changed, she was able to get a new account without eBay realizing she was the same person. As a result, she says, "guess who got a new account and re-cultivated their unsustainable eBay addiction?"[39]

Increased Convenience

Beck's experience is not unusual; many people spend more money on any number of things than they can afford. But the Internet has made this even easier, putting tempting purchases just a mouse click away. As Charles Tran, founder of the credit website CreditDonkey, says, "With all of the convenient shopping options on the web, who wouldn't start buying more online?"[40] He notes that shoppers can even save their payment information online so that they do not have to enter credit card numbers every time they buy something. Returning merchandise has also become easier, and transactions have become smoother. As a result, online shopping has increased dramatically over the past ten years. Tran says, "Since popular online shopping brands like Amazon are over a decade old, the public has a deep-seated trust in them that blends to other, smaller online retailers. It's no longer the Wild West. So people are buying more and more stuff online."[41]

Indeed, according to the statistics website Statista, in 2012 re-

The proliferation of online sellers such as Amazon and the ease of making online purchases coincide with increasing numbers of people saying they are addicted to shopping online. For some people, shopping fills a void or provides distraction from the stress and difficulties of daily life.

tail shopping websites made more than $186 billion. The number of shopping addicts appears to have gone up accordingly. In one Stanford University study, about 6 percent of women and 5.5 percent of men had what the study called a compulsive buying disorder—which the study defined as an irresistible and often senseless urge to buy something—whether online or offline. Terrence Shulman, the founder and director of the Shulman Center for Compulsive Theft, Spending & Hoarding, says this number is closer to 10 percent today.

Types of Shoppers

While an addiction to online shopping does not sound as serious as an addiction to, say, drugs or alcohol, it often starts for many of the same reasons. "Many people try to use shopping as others use drugs, alcohol or food to fill a void, numb pain, or distract themselves from stress or difficult life issues," Shulman says. "Our culture encourages shopping and once a shopaholic gets going, it's hard to stop it, especially with TV and Internet shopping. It can be like crack cocaine."[42]

Some researchers doubt that online shopping poses problems to the same degree that shopping in person in brick-and-mortar stores does, because online shopping does not provide a tactile experience. Donald Black, a professor of psychiatry at the University of Iowa who also studies impulse-control disorders, says, "One of the things compulsive shoppers will tell you is they really enjoy the shopping experience, and I'm not sure that Internet shopping provides them with the sensual pleasures they're looking for. They like the sounds, the smells, the feel of fabrics—you can't have that shopping online."[43]

Nonetheless, other experts note that not all compulsive shoppers are focused on the tactile experiences associated with shopping. Some people just want to acquire a certain number and/or kind of items. For this reason, experts are increasingly using different terms for different kinds of shopping behavior. For example, the Shulman Center provides the following terms and definitions for types of shopping addicts:

- Compulsive shoppers—shop to distract feelings; "when the going gets tough, the tough go shopping."
- Trophy shoppers—find the perfect accessory for outfits, etc. High class items will do.
- Image shoppers—pick up tab, expensive cars, highly visible stuff.
- Bargain shoppers—buy stuff they don't need just because it is a good deal. Out for the hunt.
- Codependent shoppers—to gain love and approval.
- Bulimic Shoppers—buy and return, buy and return (similar to actual bulimia [an eating disorder involving eating and purging]).
- Collector Shoppers—have to have complete or many sets of objects or different colors of same style of clothing.[44]

Serious Debt

All of these types of shopping, offline or online, can have a serious impact on the addict and his or her family. As Lorrin Koran, a professor of psychiatry and behavioral sciences at Stanford University, says, "Compulsive buying leads to serious psychological, financial, and family problems including depression, overwhelming debt and the breakup of relationships."[45] For the most extreme cases of compulsive shopping, access to the Internet can make these problems much worse.

A prominent example of this involves Buzz Bissinger, author of the 1990 best seller *Friday Night Lights*. In an essay for *GQ* magazine in April 2013, he confessed to having had a serious shopping addiction over the previous two and a half years—one that led him to spend more than $638,000 before he admitted he had a problem. His addiction focused on clothing, and he blames its onset in 2010 in large part on "the boom in online purchasing and increasingly sophisticated websites." When he discovered these sites, his writing was not going well, and as a way to avoid both the work and his anxieties toward the work, he increasingly engaged in "nasty guillotine rants on Twitter going after everything and everyone, Googling my name six or seven times a day, craving crumbs of attention. Then I started looking at clothing, hot and beautiful and transformative, a new sense of self-expression."[46]

Bissinger quickly became obsessed with buying clothing, and each purchase only made his obsession worse. He says:

> The ritual became the same: online bingeing timed to any mood, feeling anxious, feeling depressed, feeling flat, feeling excited, and desperately wanting another excitement hit. . . . I went on favorite websites day and night. . . . I purchased in the morning when I should have been writing, and it did ramp me up to help me write. I purchased in bed at night, happy that the melancholia of the day was over and I had somehow gotten through it and deserved a little extra. If there was an item that I had somehow warded off in the morning, I bought it. If something caught my eye, gave me the slightest rush, I hit the "purchase now"

button. I bought with my cell phone while waiting to have lunch with someone, or dinner, or a drink. I bought while I was *having* lunch with someone, or dinner, or a drink, happy when they went to the bathroom so I could finish the transaction without interruption.[47]

Bissinger says he was excited whenever the doorbell rang, because it meant a package was being delivered, and for him the

An Addiction to Selling

Just as some people can become addicted to buying things online, so too can people become addicted to selling things online. Jill Smokler, an author of books related to parenting, was once such an addict. Several years ago she was obsessed with selling things on eBay, to the point that she eventually started searching for things to sell. On her website she reports:

> From the moment I sold my first pair of jeans, I was *hooked*. I went to bed thinking about what I could list [for sale] next and woke up ready to photograph, write, and post my listings. My dining room table was [an] assembly line of boxes, bubble wrap and tape. I bought a postal scale and formed a tight bond with the postman who appeared at my door daily to pick up my newest sales. I systematically went through every [item] in my house, making piles of the best things to sell. . . . I sold old clothes, old books, my wedding crystal and stemware. . . . I sold *everything*. . . . When I had run out of things to sell around the house, I started buying things just to sell.

Jill Smokler, "The eBay Addiction." Scary Mommy, 2013. www.scarymommy.com.

opening of a package was a tactile experience as powerful as buying something in a store. He explains:

> I received a package at least every other day and sometimes two or three or four. Because I ordered so much, I often forgot what was inside them. It added to the drama and the ritual: the slice of the Swiss Army knife down the spine of the cardboard box and then the quick cuts along each side, the greedy pulling out of the paper stuffing, the annoyance of having to unzip the inevitable garment bag because it took too much . . . time, and then holding the item aloft on its hanger with thrill and titillation.[48]

Online Auctions

Many other online shoppers, including those who frequent online auction sites, report experiencing this same kind of thrill. However, the thrill of online auctions might have more to do with the rush people get when they compete with others for an item than from the actual purchase. This might not be a problem until people start buying items they do not need and cannot afford. As psychologist Kimberly S. Young notes, "It gets more serious when eBay addicts feel a sense of accomplishment when they are the highest bidder and begin to bid on items they don't need."[49]

People who are obsessed with online auction sites such as eBay often feel the need to continually check the last seconds of auctions to make sure they are not outbid. Some even search for auctions about to end so that they can experience the thrill of outbidding other participants. Young reports that some of the people she has treated have been fired from their jobs for spending time on eBay when they should have been working. Others have taken huge financial and personal risks to continue their obsessive activities. She recalls one patient who was already in debt by $400,000 when she took out a second mortgage on her home and withdrew the money from her retirement account in order to continue funding her eBay addiction—all while

"I received a package at least every other day and sometimes two or three or four. Because I ordered so much, I often forgot what was inside them."[48]

— Author Buzz Bissinger on his online shopping addiction.

trying to keep her activities a secret from her husband. Such actions and deceptions are not uncommon, Young says.

Social Activities

Online shopping, then, typically involves separating from and competing against others. In contrast, social networking is about trying to connect with others, and some people become just as obsessive about making these connections as an eBay addict does about checking auctions. According to a 2012 survey by Boost Mobile, 68 percent of people aged sixteen to twenty-five admitted checking their social media feeds or sites up to ten times a day. In addition, people aged fifteen to nineteen spent an average of three hours a day on social media, and those aged twenty to twenty-nine spent an average of two hours doing this. More than 90 percent of those surveyed by Boost Mobile reported that Facebook was their most-used form of social media, and many other studies have found Facebook to have a similar degree of popularity. Conse-

The thrill of bidding and winning keeps some people coming back again and again to online auction sites such as eBay. Those who continually bid on items they do not need or cannot afford may be experiencing a form of addiction.

quently, most research into social media addiction has focused on the use of Facebook, which is why social media addiction is most commonly talked about in terms of Facebook addiction.

Among the most prominent studies of Facebook addiction is a research project headed by Cecilie Schou Andreassen, a psycholo-

Facebook Envy

In January 2013 a study conducted at the Technical University of Darmstadt, a research university in the city of Darmstadt, Germany, showed that using Facebook can trigger negative feelings strong enough to cause emotional damage. This study examined the reactions that people had when reading posts sharing good news and viewing photographs in which others were clearly happy. One in three test subjects experienced extreme envy or jealousy, with vacation photos causing the highest amount of resentment. Among subjects in their mid-thirties and forties, envy was most often experienced by women who were exposed to photographs or posts that demonstrated family happiness or physical attractiveness in others. Images of family happiness also sometimes provoked loneliness. A previous study, reported in December 2012, had similar results, showing that the more time college students spent on Facebook, the worse they felt about their own lives.

However, Facebook can lead to positive emotions as well. Research conducted at Cornell University in 2011 found that college students demonstrated an increase in self-esteem after reading friends' positive responses to things they themselves had shared on their Facebook wall. They received a similar boost from scrolling down their Facebook wall to view pictures they themselves had previously posted.

gist at the University of Bergen in Norway, who has found that Facebook addicts are typically uncomfortable with face-to-face interactions. She says that "people who are anxious and socially insecure use Facebook more than those with lower scores on those traits, probably because those who are anxious find it easier to communicate via social media than face-to-face."[50] Her studies have also found that Facebook addiction occurs more often among young people than among older people, and that people who are more organized and more ambitious are less likely to succumb to Facebook addiction than others.

To help health professionals assess whether someone is suffering from Facebook addiction, Andreassen's research team developed the Facebook Addiction Scale in collaboration with the Bergen Clinics Foundation. This scale is based on six criteria rated according to whether they occur very rarely, rarely, sometimes, often, or very often; four or more items rated as occurring more than sometimes indicates a Facebook addiction. According to the University of Bergen, these criteria are:

- You spend a lot of time thinking about Facebook or plan use of Facebook.
- You feel an urge to use Facebook more and more.
- You use Facebook in order to forget about personal problems.
- You have tried to cut down on the use of Facebook without success.
- You become restless or troubled if you are prohibited from using Facebook.
- You use Facebook so much that it has had a negative impact on your job/studies.[51]

As with online shopping addiction, addiction to social networking sites like Facebook can have a serious negative impact on addicts' lives. As an example, psychologist Jeremy Dean cites the case of a twenty-four-year-old woman who sought help from a psychiatric clinic in Athens, Greece. He reports:

She had joined Facebook eight months previously, and

since then, her life had taken a nosedive. She told doctors she had 400 online friends and spent five hours a day on her Facebook page. She recently lost her job as a waitress because she kept sneaking out to visit a nearby Internet cafe. She wasn't sleeping properly and was feeling anxious. As though to underline the problem, during the clinical interview she took out her mobile phone and tried to check her Facebook page.[52]

The fact that this woman's problem developed within just eight months is not unusual. Diana Bocco, who writes about issues related to Internet communications, notes that when it comes to online addiction, "things can escalate quickly." She explains:

> One reason these sites are so addictive is that there's a nonstop stream of messages, photos, updates and information coming from those in your network. If you have 10 friends, it shouldn't be a problem keeping up with them. If your

Despite the alluring bay view along the mouth of the Amazon River in Brazil, a tourist spends her time checking her Facebook page. According to the Facebook Addiction Scale, this behavior might be considered a sign of a person who is addicted to Facebook.

network is 100 friends or more, you might end up online for hours every day, trying to check all of the updates. If you're trading messages back and forth with other members, you might find yourself even more caught up in the exchange, just as you would in a normal conversation.[53]

Affecting Sleep

It is also not unusual for people to lose sleep over social networking. A March 2010 study by the consumer electronics group Retrevo, which relied on interviews with one thousand adults in the United States, found that 48 percent of those surveyed updated and/or read Facebook or Twitter whenever they woke up in the night and as soon as they woke up in the morning. In addition, 28 percent of those who used iPhones to access the Internet in the morning did not even wait until they got out of bed to check their Facebook or Twitter accounts. Some individuals even confessed to doing this while in the bathroom or in the middle of romantic interactions.

Research has also shown that sometimes a person will have trouble controlling Internet use when it comes to one social networking site but not another. For example, Laurel Snyder, an author in Atlanta, Georgia, became obsessed only with Twitter. She says, "I was OK with e-mail and Facebook. But Twitter! Twitter is different. It's faster and bigger and looser. It's the biggest cocktail party in the world, 24-7." Her comparison to a cocktail party stems from Twitter's immediacy. She explains, "Twitter is unspooling in real time, and so what happened an hour ago is, well, in the past. Nobody will bother to read what you tweeted four hours ago any more than people at a get-together will overhear what happened before they got there. Like any party, if you duck in and out for a few minutes, you miss all the best parts." As a result, she says, "you don't do things with Twitter. You become a part of it."[54]

Unfortunately for Snyder, while she was obsessively reading and sending tweets, she was neglecting her family, chores, and

"One reason these sites are so addictive is that there's a nonstop stream of messages, photos, updates and information coming from those in your network."[53]

— Diana Bocco, an expert on Internet communications.

work—and yet this was not what made her realize she had a problem. Instead, it was her response to a temporary unavailability of the Twitter website and related services. She reports, "I stared at the blank screen, hitting refresh over and over. Waiting for everyone to come back. For my online life to resume."[55] She spent the rest of the day obsessively thinking about Twitter, and by the time the service was restored, she knew she had an addiction to fight.

A Part of Daily Life

However, Snyder also knew she could not abandon the Internet altogether, and she did not think she needed to. She says:

> Twitter, and Facebook, and googlechat, and e-mail and whatever comes next are not drugs, though they can become unhealthy. They're daily tools, part of the world we live in. I really do need to communicate with people, check my calendar, pay my bills. I need to e-mail my editor daily, and there's no way around that. I can't move to a cabin in Wyoming and send letters by homing pigeon. Instead, I have to find a kind of moderation. I have to find a balance. Which, for this week anyway, is taking the form of keeping track of my time. I am allowing myself no more than an hour online each day. I am using a stupid egg timer, and only replying to work-related e-mails. Which feels silly, childish, but that's the price I pay for my overdose.[56]

"*Twitter, and Facebook, and googlechat, and e-mail and whatever comes next are not drugs, though they can become unhealthy. They're daily tools, part of the world we live in.*"[56]

— Former social media addict Laurel Snyder.

Using an egg timer to keep track of time might feel silly, but experts say that sometimes such steps are necessary because the Internet can cause users to lose track of time. As a participant in a study on how the Internet affects one's sense of time explains, "If I really get into something then, you know, I suddenly look at my watch and it's like two hours later and I don't know where the time has gone, but that's from just concentrating so much that you don't really know what's going on around you. My colleague actually said that I needed to go for a hearing test, I'm just completely transfixed."[57]

Social networking is particularly problematic in this regard, because it encourages users to search the Internet for information, websites, and photos they can share with friends. While surfing, many people get lost in the web, following one link after another to site after site, oblivious to their surroundings. This kind of oblivious state is generally referred to as flow, a state of consciousness that occurs when a person is engaged in an activity so absorbing that all sense of time is lost.

A study into Internet-caused flow at the University of the Witwatersrand in South Africa found that it was most often triggered by social activities, particularly an online chat followed by blogging. The study also found that if the person engaging in such activities while experiencing flow was also using the Internet in order to avoid doing serious work, then that person was more likely to develop an Internet addiction. In other words, social activities plus procrastination plus flow equal what the researchers called PIU—Problematic Internet Use. The study's authors concluded:

> The results give strong support for the contention that the online activities that are most interactive (i.e. online games, online chat, online telephony, and blogging) are the best predictors of PIU, flow on the Internet and Internet procrastination. . . . These online activities each have a number of qualities in common including high degrees of social interaction, perceived control, and they are intrinsically motivating, and absorbing.[58]

In writing about this study, Timothy A. Pychyl, a professor of psychology at Carleton University in Ottawa, Canada, notes that this research shows the importance of monitoring the time one spends on ordinary Internet communication. He says:

> It's important to remember how seductive and potentially problematic the Internet can be. Although it's easy to identify cyber-crime (downloading or distributing illegal material, hacking, online sexual harassment or child por-

"It's important to remember how seductive and potentially problematic the Internet can be."[59]

— Timothy A. Pychyl, a professor of psychology at Carleton University in Ottawa, Canada.

nography) as a problem area for the Internet, the more mundane effects on our ability to self-regulate are equally important. Many Web . . . applications in particular provide control, ease of use, immediate feedback, interactivity and access to entertainment that make it likely that a flow experience may well be developed in relation to activities that we never really intended to invest our time in. Learning to recognize the features of the problem is a first step to maintaining our self-regulatory ability.[59]

Whenever a person cannot self-regulate Internet use, that person risks losing time and, in severe cases of PIU, losing money and threatening or even destroying relationships as well.

Facts

- Experts in the field of Internet addiction generally say that spending thirty-eight hours or more a week on the computer is a sign of a serious problem.

- Go-Globe.com states that based on the number of hours that Facebook users spent online in 2012, more than 350 million Facebook users suffer from Facebook addiction syndrome.

- In May 2013 Facebook reported that 1.1 billion people use the site each month.

- According to a 2012 survey by Boost Mobile, it is not uncommon for people who have one thousand Facebook friends to check their Facebook page fifty times or more throughout the day.

- The *Search Engine Journal* reports that the social media site Pinterest, which was launched in 2010 and had 10.4 million users by the end of 2012, is the fastest-growing social media site in history, often increasing its number of users by 400 percent from one month to the next.

- Infographics Labs reports that in 2012 there were 175 million tweets sent daily from Twitter.

- According to researchers at the Stanford University School of Medicine, compulsive buyers are more likely to report having incomes under $50,000 and more than four times as likely as other people to make only the minimum payment on credit card balances.

- As of 2012 Facebook had more than five hundred groups devoted to discussing social networking addictions.

Are Addictions to Gaming and Gambling Serious Problems?

Long before there was an Internet, people sometimes had trouble limiting the time they spent playing video games and gambling. But studies have suggested that the Internet has made these activities more addictive than ever, largely because it provides easy and immediate access to games and opponents. For example, researchers at Nottingham Trent University in the United Kingdom have found that 0.5 percent of people who only gamble offline can be considered to have a serious gambling problem, whereas 5 percent of online gamblers can be considered addicted to gambling. Similarly, studies have shown that people who stick to playing video games offline typically play an average of six hours a week, whereas the typical online gamer plays roughly twenty-five hours a week. Moreover, more than one out of ten of these online players exceeds forty hours a week of game play.

DiAnn Edwards of Red Lion, Pennsylvania, is an example of someone who falls into the most extreme category of game player.

This fifty-one-year-old housewife plays *Farmville* on her laptop up to eight hours a day and spends $200 a month on various purchases related to the game. She says of this behavior, "It just gets addicting. I'm 51 and what am I doing sitting here playing a Farmville game? I don't get it, but it actually drives me crazy."[60]

Designed to be part of Facebook and therefore categorized as a social game, *Farmville* has well over 80 million active users. Players are in the role of farmers, and as such they plow the land, plant crops, and acquire buildings, fences, animals, and other things for their farms. To get the virtual money for farm expenses and purchases, they can "sell" harvested crops. Items can also be gifted from one player to another, and doing chores to earn experience or completing certain achievements can unlock items and allow players to ascend in game level.

For some people, these activities can be surprisingly addictive. In a Facebook discussion group on the issue, one *Farmville* player posted, "When you go to sleep you dream about your farm or lay there half the night thinking how to rearrange your farm for more space and getting up three hours before work just to farm."[61] Another said, "You sit in your car with your laptop in front of the community college so you can use their wifi connection (which is faster than your broadband at home). So what if it's 30 degrees outside? I've got crops to harvest!"[62] Still another complained:

> My mom's addicted. It's not fun. She's always playing and gets slightly rude about it. She seriously needs help. Farm Ville is ruining my mom and while she spends her time on FARM VILLE she COULD have been helping me write, but she apparently thinks that taking care of a farm on the internet is more important than helping her daughter do the dishes, or help her with homework. There should be a real Farm Ville addict group. I think my mom seriously needs help.[63]

Dr. Timothy Fong, who runs a clinic for behavioral addiction at the University of California–Los Angeles, says of women like this, "The stereotype of the 'videogame addict' is a teenage kid in his underwear. That's not what's happening out there. The average

More than 80 million active Facebook users play the game Farmville *(pictured). Some players say they think about the game day and night; others have become so preoccupied with the game that they have lost track of daily needs.*

age of our patients is about 40. We've seen housewives, doctors, lawyers."[64] In fact, according to a survey commissioned by game maker Popcap Games, the average social gamer is a forty-three-year-old woman; 55 percent of social gamers are female, and 45 percent are male.

Fong also reports that video games can trigger compulsive behavior that is just as extreme as the behavior exhibited by people addicted to drugs or alcohol. He says, "It's the same exact clinical symptoms: preoccupation, loss of control, inability to stop. They keep playing the game despite harmful consequences so, in my mind, absolutely I believe it is the same disease as alcohol or drug addiction."[65]

Ultimate Control?

The kind of harmful consequences gaming addicts face varies according to the degree of the addiction. However, even a mild addiction can cause problems at work and at home. Shannon Chrismore of the Illinois Institute for Addiction Recovery, which has a treatment course devoted to video game addiction, says that many such addicts leave work early or go into work late in order to have more time for gaming, and their gaming is hurting their personal relationships as well. In extreme cases of addiction, she adds, "they are skipping social engagements, hygiene has gone down the drain, they have not showered, have not moved and they're not eating appropriately."[66] A former addict, Jason Ramsey, has noted this kind of behavior among fellow gamers. He says, "I've seen so many things fall through for these people because of these stupid games. It blows my mind that people don't have that self control."[67]

An example of a severe loss of self-control in regard to online gaming is the case of Ryan G. Van Cleave. A university English professor, he first had a problem with video gaming about a decade ago, when he was late taking his then pregnant wife to a doctor's appointment because he was busy playing an online sports game. Then he discovered the game *World of Warcraft*, at a time in his life when he was unhappy with his job and stressed out at home. This game took him away from his troubles and made him feel successful. As he later wrote in his book *Unplugged: My Journey in the Dark World of Video Game Addiction*, "Playing WoW [*World of Warcraft*] makes me feel god-like. I have ultimate control and can do what I want with few real repercussions. The real world makes me feel impotent. . . . A computer malfunction, a sobbing child, a suddenly dead cellphone battery—the littlest hitch in daily living feels profoundly disempowering."[68]

> "I've seen so many things fall through for these people because of these stupid games. It blows my mind that people don't have that self control."[67]
>
> — Former gaming addict Jason Ramsey about current addicts.

Van Cleave spent entire weekends playing the game. He began neglecting his wife and children and would sneak in games during the middle of the night and while relatives were visiting. Soon Van Cleave was feeling estranged from his coworkers as well. He says, "All that tethered me to anything meaningful during this time was WoW, which I clung to for dear life."[69]

When the contract on his full-time teaching job was not renewed, he was forced to take a part-time position. This provided him with even more time for gaming, and his addiction escalated.

Six Criteria for a Gaming Addiction

Experts disagree on the behaviors that constitute an addiction to gaming. However, many use criteria based on a model developed by psychologist Iain Brown of the University of Glasgow in Scotland in the late 1990s. It has six features that, if present for a significant amount of time, can indicate that someone has an addiction. In regard to gaming, these would be (1) salience, which occurs when gaming becomes the most important activity in a person's life; (2) mood modification, whereby a person's mood changes, in a way the gamer considers positive, as a direct result of playing a game; (3) tolerance, whereby the gamer needs to play more and more often, for longer and longer periods, in order to achieve the same mood-changing results; (4) withdrawal, whereby the gamer suffers negative feelings and/or physical effects as a result of reducing or stopping gaming; (5) relapse, whereby the gamer quickly returns to gaming after a period of reduction or abstinence; and (6) harm, which is any kind of negative effect on the gamer's life as a result of gaming, such as family problems, job loss, or suicidal thoughts.

As a result, he says, "My kids hate me. My wife is threatening (again) to leave me. I haven't written anything in countless months. I have no prospects for the next academic year. And I am perpetually exhausted from skipping sleep so I can play more Warcraft."[70]

Three years into his *World of Warcraft* addiction, on a night in December 2007 after he had played the game for eighteen hours straight, Van Cleave stood on a bridge contemplating suicide. The thought frightened him so much that he went home and uninstalled the game from his computer. After that he experienced what he believes were withdrawal symptoms—headaches, stomachaches, anxiety attacks—but he did not reinstall the game. At the peak of his addiction, he had been playing more than sixty hours a week, and he decided he never wanted to suffer through that again.

Rewarding Behavior

Some people cite the fact that Van Cleave was able to quit his addiction abruptly and without help—although not without distress—as evidence that he was not really addicted. In fact, they argue that it is impossible to be addicted to gaming, saying that this activity results not from a compulsion but from a strong temptation based on pleasant memories of the behavior. But other experts say that rewards rather than memories are at the heart of the desire to play games and that these rewards are what make gaming potentially addictive.

With all games, winning is the ultimate reward, but often there are also prizes and the acquisition of virtual money along the way. In describing this aspect of *World of Warcraft*, Van Cleave says, "There was always something better and cooler. You can never have enough in-game money, enough armour, enough support."[71]

However, these rewards are not given consistently. Each player's *World of Warcraft* game character, also called an avatar or toon, has to perform quests and other activities in cooperation with other players' characters in order to obtain virtual items that are beneficial within the game. But certain awards and prizes are not given consistently. For example, sometimes a nonplaying character—a character controlled not by a human player but by the game—does not provide a piece of armor or weapon when expected. This random reward system has an impact on how much people want to continue playing the game.

Psychologists have long known that rewarding people for a behavior at a variable rate, where the reward is not obviously and immediately forthcoming, can increase their desire to engage in that behavior. Game designers know this as well, so they incorporate variable payoffs into their games in order to encourage repeat play. Consequently, game designer Andrea Phillips

"It's that tension of knowing you might get the treat, but not knowing exactly when, that keeps you playing. The player develops an unshakeable faith, after a while, that THIS will be the time I hit it big."[72]

— Game designer Andrea Phillips on intermittent rewards.

says, "It's that tension of knowing you might get the treat, but not knowing exactly when, that keeps you playing. The player develops an unshakeable faith, after a while, that THIS will be the time I hit it big. THIS is the time it will all pay off, no matter how many times it hasn't so far. Just one more turn. One more minute. But it's really never just one more."[72]

Games of Skill and Chance

Intermittent rewards are also what make online gambling more addictive than many other online activities. As psychologist John M. Grohol notes, "Checking e-mail . . . is not the same as pulling a slot-machine's handle. One is social seeking behavior, the other is reward seeking behavior. They are two very different things, as any behaviorist will tell you."[73]

Slot machines are programmed to keep a certain percentage of the money fed into them as profit for the owner of the machines and then pay out the rest to players. If instead of these rewards being intermittent, every play rewarded the gambler with ninety cents for every dollar put into the machine, for example, the gambler would soon get bored and stop playing. But because every time a dollar is put into the machine there is a chance of getting many times that dollar back as a reward, people keep playing—even though it is far more likely they will get nothing in exchange for their money.

Games that involve skill as well as chance can be even more seductive, and when it comes to online gaming one of the most popular of these is poker. At any one time, day or night, there are thousands of online poker games going on, involving players from all over the world. The number of entrants into these games, many of which are tournaments, vary from as few as ten to as many as several thousand. In some, players gamble virtual money; in others, real money.

The hosts of poker rooms typically make money from players in the form of rakes, which are an amount of money taken from each pot (all the money bet on a hand), and from fees charged to

> "Checking e-mail . . . is not the same as pulling a slot-machine's handle. One is social seeking behavior, the other is reward seeking behavior."[73]
>
> — Psychologist John M. Grohol.

enter games and tournaments. Thus, the more players there are on a website, the more revenues there are for those running the site's games. Consequently, many sites offer monetary bonuses to attract players (such as twenty dollars for depositing one hundred dollars in an account of money to be spent on game play). But since these bonuses are typically awarded only after the gambler has played a certain predetermined number of raked hands, this serves to encourage an addiction to the site.

Poker Addictions

But even sites that do not offer bonuses can be highly addictive, because online poker has many features that make it hard for gamblers to stop playing. Gamblers typically play in the privacy of their own homes, which means there is often no one around to urge them to stop playing after a big loss. Players who lose all

Poker players can find online games at all times of the day or night. Some say online gambling is highly addictive because it is fun and fast; additionally, because it can be done in the privacy of one's own home, play can continue around the clock.

their money in a game can easily transfer more into their gambling account using credit cards or online money transfers—and the temptation to keep playing to try to recoup losses is strong. Consequently, Josh Axelrad, a professional blackjack player who became hooked on online poker, calls online gambling "the perfect vehicle for addiction." He explains, "You never have to stop (you don't need to go home when you are home); it's private (your problems are easy to hide); and it plays at a riveting, breakneck speed. Casinos are a snore by comparison."[74]

Axelrad had been very successful as a blackjack player, winning more than $700,000 for himself and friends over a period of five years. But as an online poker addict, he could not control his betting in the same way. From the spring of 2005 to September 2006, he lost approximately $50,000 gambling at online poker sites, and as a result, he says:

> I bore the additional expense of lost time, lost pride, of disorientation and fear. Beginning—as addictions will—casually, poker changed me, and before I dropped the first 10k I was dependent on the feelings it delivered. I felt alive only when I was in action. Soon I needed to rescue myself from the pitfall I'd created but could not accept. I'd lost so much money. Poker became the solution; I couldn't stop to wonder what the problem might be.[75]

Growing Numbers

Such problems are particularly worrisome among young people, who might be starting their futures in massive debt because of gambling problems. According to the National Council on Problem Gambling, in 2012, 75 percent of college students and 60 to 80 percent of high school students reported having gambled for money during the past year. Moreover, young people suffer from problem gambling at a rate two to three times higher than do adults. One reason for this is that students often need or want money, so they are initially drawn to gambling in the hopes of winning it big—and many of them are unaware of how high the odds are stacked against this. Another reason, studies suggest, is

Computer-Related Injuries

Using a computer for hours at a time can cause a variety of physical injuries. The most common are overuse injuries involving hands, wrists, and elbows, whereby repetitive motions like clicking a mouse can cause damage and inflammation in tendons, nerve sheaths, and ligaments. Computer gamers are particularly susceptible to repetitive-motion injuries, and the result is painful muscles and tendons, swelling, stiffness in joints, and weakness and numbness in the afflicted parts of the body. Poor posture can also cause back, neck, and shoulder pains, and staring at a screen for too long can lead to eyestrain.

Excessive computer use can cause another type of physical harm as well: obesity. Many Internet addicts have poor eating habits as a result of being unwilling to take time away from the computer in order to cook and eat healthy foods. Internet addicts also get little exercise other than clicking a mouse. Consequently, studies have shown that reducing the computer time of overweight children by half results in significant weight loss.

that young people think they are better at playing games like poker than they really are and will have no trouble beating other players.

Still another reason is the ease with which someone too young to gamble legally can engage in online gambling. Casinos strictly enforce age limits; gambling websites rarely do. As the website StateUniversity.com reports: "Online gambling only takes a credit card or debit card and an Internet connection. This pretty much puts every college student at risk. In practice, there is no age limitation on online gambling because there is no true age identification process. One study found that out of 37 randomly selected online gambling sites, a minor was able to register, play, and pay at 30 of them."[76]

Studies have also shown that among young people, males are far more likely than females to gamble and to experience gambling problems. However, surveys indicate that the Internet is increasingly drawing to gambling women who would never have gambled in offline venues. Some suggest that the number of women with gambling problems has doubled in recent years. Studies also indicate that men are initially attracted to gambling out of a desire to beat competitors, feel powerful and successful, and acquire money, whereas women often gamble for emotional reasons. Liz Karter, an addiction counselor for GamCare, a nonprofit group that offers support for gambling addicts, says:

> When it comes to women, we often see gambling as a symptom of someone's underlying emotional distress. You do see from time to time a woman coming forward who is using gambling as a means of escape from the stresses that modern life puts on her, the demands of a job, children, her partner, her financial responsibilities. . . . But more often I see women who have had some traumatic experience, like an abusive relationship and they feel quite bad about themselves so they shut everything out by gambling. You hear them say "I'm in a bubble, I'm in a trance."[77]

Karter also notes that unlike an addiction to alcohol, an addiction to online gambling does not make it physically difficult to care for children while the gambling is going on. Nonetheless, the children of online gamblers can still suffer because gambling addicts are often emotionally detached from loved ones. The gamblers can suffer as well, losing not only time and money but self-respect, and many feel so ashamed of their actions that they go to great lengths to hide their addictions from loved ones. Unfortunately for these people, this shame can prevent them from seeking help for their addictions when they are unable on their own to stop gaming or gambling.

Facts

- According to the HowStuffWorks website, there are currently more than two hundred Internet poker rooms online.

- HowStuffWorks reports that the largest Internet poker room has more than fifty thousand people playing at the same time during peak playing hours.

- Surveys have shown that women are more likely than men to play social games with people they know than with strangers.

- Surveys have shown that the average gamer has played six social games and more than half of gamers started playing a game because a friend played it.

- According to SuperData Research, the most popular online social gambling games in 2013 were poker (28.15 percent), casino table games (24.26 percent), slot machines (21.67 percent), and bingo (11.3 percent).

- According to the online gaming industry, 42 percent of online gamers are female.

How Can People Recover from Online Addictions?

A group called Internet Addicts Anonymous formed in New York in 2008 using Alcoholics Anonymous (AA), the group for recovering alcoholics, as its model. That model includes a twelve-step program—a guiding set of principles outlining a course of action for recovery. The founder of Internet Addicts Anonymous, an Internet addict named Pauline, envisioned that members would go to regular meetings to help support one another through the problems of ending an addiction. With this support, she thought, individuals would be able to conquer their addictions on their own instead of relying on therapy or formal treatment programs, both of which could be expensive.

To this end she posted a notice online telling when and where her group would meet, but no more than four people ever showed up to any of her meetings. None of them had the exact same type of Internet addiction, making support more difficult; it was hard for someone addicted to viewing pornography online, for example, to understand what someone addicted to online gambling was going through. Consequently, after ten meetings Pauline shut down the group, even though it had been unique enough to attract media attention.

A Lifetime of Struggles

Even without her group, however, Pauline has managed to control her tendency to overuse the Internet, after a lifetime of struggling with it. Pauline's troubles began in high school, when she would go online over and over again to check for e-mail. In college this behavior intensified, and she also succumbed to the lure of a few basic computer games. Because this occurred in the late 1990s, though, the computer she used was in her college's computer lab instead of her dorm room, which served to limit her behavior somewhat.

After she graduated and got an office job, her addiction worsened. She reports:

> I found myself constantly reading blogs, checking email, chatting, and even playing games. Even when I had more work than I could possibly finish, even when things got to be late. I started to get in trouble for not getting enough work done. One of the worst parts, though, was hard to measure. I found myself getting worse at paying attention, at focusing. Someone would call me on the phone and ask me to do something, but before I did it I'd check in on a blog, which led to another blog . . . and I'd totally forget about the phone call. Or any time I had a spare minute, which might have been used for thinking about my overall workload, I'd be on the internet instead. So the only work I'd ever do would be the emergencies. I had no sense of the overall structure of my working life. At home, I'd often be up long past when I needed to go to sleep, doing useless things on the internet, promising myself I'd shut down in just 5 more minutes . . . again and again and again.[78]

Finally things got so bad that she visited a therapist, who worked with her to try to help her minimize her computer time. No matter what Pauline tried, however, she just could not limit her Internet use. For example, one of her therapist's suggestions was that she use the computer only for personal activities at work during her lunch hour, and then for every minute she went over that hour, she was supposed to stay late to pay her employer back for the stolen time. Instead, on certain evenings she found herself playing around on the Internet when she still had time to pay back but could not stay any later at the office.

Given such failures, her therapist finally told her that she was too addicted to handle using the Internet at all. She would have to quit her job, he said, and find another that did not involve computers. Unwilling to do this, in desperation she called a friend who was in AA, and he suggested she treat her Internet addiction as though it were an alcohol addiction, following the twelve steps and taking her recovery one day at a time. As a result, she was able to control her addiction for six months. She describes this period as some of the best months of her life, adding, "It's hard to explain how much clearer everything is when you're not on the internet all the time. But it made my life better in every part. Not just work, but in my social life, my love life, my experience of the world. I even slept better—not just longer, but better."[79] Unfortunately for Pauline, she then had a relapse, so she decided that she needed AA-style meetings to get back on track.

Cognitive Behavioral Therapy

Today Pauline is once again managing to control her addiction, but she no longer works in an office, and she has to monitor her behavior constantly. She sometimes still plays online games, but if she finds herself spending too much time on any one game, she deletes it to make sure she stops playing. She considers herself a recovering Internet addict—able to manage her addiction but not free of it.

Others do not feel capable of taking even these steps. Some Internet addicts seek out therapy as way of dealing with their addiction. Internet addiction expert Kimberly S. Young conducted a study in which she found that a particular type of therapy, cognitive behavioral therapy (CBT), was particularly successful. By the eighth session, most of her 114 study participants were able to manage their addiction symptoms, and this management was sustained during a six-month follow-up period. In another study

conducted at the Shanghai Medical Center in China, fifty-six pa-tients aged twelve to seventeen were divided into two groups—twenty-four in a control group that experienced no treatment and thirty-two in a group that received eight sessions of CBT. Both groups demonstrated a decrease in Internet use, but the CBT group showed greater improvement in time-management skills as well as improved emotional states and the ability to manage un-wanted behaviors.

CBT is a type of short-term therapy that helps people identify problematic thought patterns and change them for the better. It is used to treat a wide variety of psychological disorders, including mood, anxiety, personality, eating, and substance abuse disorders. The theory behind this approach to therapy is that thoughts and feelings are instrumental in driving behavior and that emotional and behavioral responses are learned and can be unlearned. When CBT is used to treat addiction, patients are taught to recognize

One woman started an online addiction support group in New York similar to Alcoholics Anonymous. The group did not last, but some experts say therapy can help people who are addicted to online activities.

situations in which they are most likely to be tempted to engage in unwanted behavior and to avoid these situations if possible. They also learn techniques to help them cope with such situations if avoidance is not possible. In addition, therapists talk to patients about how they felt prior to having the addiction and about what feelings and circumstances led to and developed because of the addiction. Such discussions are designed to help patients avoid relapsing after kicking the addiction.

Exploring Feelings

Former online shopping addict Kate Abbott is one of those helped by this kind of therapy. At her first session with her therapist, she was asked how she would feel if she *couldn't* shop. She says that at first she did not see the point of this question, but gradually it led her to an awareness of what her real problem was: not the things she was buying, but the emotions associated with her ability to buy them. She struggled to answer the question, as she explains:

> I imagined it: a week without being able to go online to my favorite stores, to sort through lovely items on sale, to have new things brought to me. To reward myself after or before or during a long day of invisible parenting work. To reward [my son] Henry for putting up with me as an imperfect mother. To give Henry fun things to play with because I didn't always want to play with him myself. My heart constricted. I wasn't sure I could even articulate the feeling, and I told her that, but I said, "It would make me feel . . . little. Like I'm a little kid. Like I'm not in charge." . . . And then the connections snapped together. I thought shopping helped me show myself I was an adult, that I could make my own decisions about things I liked, that Henry and I both deserved stuff as a reward for getting through trying days, and that my personality and interests weren't entirely overcome by being an at-home mom. I didn't want to feel powerless. I had money, so I could spend it. And I did.[80]

Despite this realization, her behavior did not change immediately. She had to continue to work with her therapist to control

Killing Access

When Internet addicts cannot control their computer use, sometimes others attempt to control it for them. This has occurred, for example, in cases where Facebook abuse at work has led an employer to install blocking software that will prevent access to the site on office computers. There is also software that will block access to all Internet browsers to prevent people from surfing the web while at work. Some employers also ban the use of personal cell phones at work to prevent workers from going online while on the job.

A more creative way to block access to an addictive Internet activity is an approach used by a man in China who was unhappy with his son's gaming addiction. He hired some virtual assassins to kill his twenty-three-year-old son's character in an online role-playing game over and over again whenever the young man played, so that his gaming experience was ruined.

her addiction, which prior to therapy had compelled her to spend $2,000 to $3,000 more each month than her husband earned. But she was aided by the fact that shortly after her first therapy session, someone stole her credit card number, forcing her to cut up her credit card and await a new one. This made it impossible for her to buy things online, and when she got her new card she made a point not to memorize its number or to update the number stored at her existing online shopping websites.

Treatment Centers

Abbott was able to control her addiction with the help of counseling sessions that she could fit in around her regular daily life. But some people feel they need a more intensive therapy experience. These are offered at treatment centers that specialize in helping addicts. For example, the Center for Internet and Technology Addiction in West Hartford, Connecticut, offers two- and five-day intensive outpatient treatment programs on Internet, gaming, personal device, and social media addictions. Each day lasts ten hours for the two-day program and four hours for the five-day program. These programs are designed to identify problem patterns of behavior and help patients recognize, understand, and break these patterns in order to eliminate unwanted behaviors. In addition, patients explore underlying aspects of their life that might be contributing to their addictions, including psychological issues and the dynamics of social and family relationships. They also develop a plan for moving back into their daily lives without relapsing into addiction and for addressing the beginnings of a relapse should one occur.

Although the Connecticut center is able to accomplish these things with patients on an outpatient basis, other centers require patients to live at the center for a period of weeks or months, completely cut off from all access to technology and the Internet. Young says that such an approach is unnecessary, and psychiatrist Jerald J. Block says that abruptly cutting off Internet access can even be harmful if the addiction is being used to help the sufferer deal with difficult emotions. A gradual approach, such experts say, is far better than quitting cold turkey. Nonetheless, residential centers are growing in popularity, although there are still not nearly enough to meet demand.

The first to be established in the United States was reSTART in Fall City, Washington, a 5-acre (2 ha) retreat about 30 miles (48 km) east of Seattle. The center, which opened in 1994, has been treating Internet addicts as inpatients, six patients at a time, for the past four years for a fee of $14,000 each. The treatment program lasts forty-five days, during which patients have no access to Facebook, eBay, Twitter, video games, or other potentially addictive online activities. One of reSTART's patients, former University of Iowa student Ben Alexander, was trying to kick an addiction to *World of Warcraft* when he came to the center. When his playing time reached seventeen hours a day, he dropped out of school to attend a substance abuse program as an outpatient, but because it

Sleep Problems

Studies have shown that compulsive Internet use adversely affects sleep. Dr. John Cline, an expert in sleep disorders, reports:

> I have encountered many people who are staying up most or all of the night playing on-line games. The progressive lack of sleep can diminish their ability to function at work or in school, can lead to dangerous behavior such as drowsy driving, can contribute to weight gain, and can deepen feelings of depression. And this applies to individuals other than gamers. Some may be compulsively watching Internet pornography, again resulting in loss of sleep and increasing dysfunction at work. Still others are giving up sleep to spend hours on-line interacting with friends or acquaintances on Facebook. Sometimes people will use caffeine pills or other stimulants to stay awake late into the night. Functioning and health suffer when sleep is sacrificed night after night in compulsive web surfing.

These problems, Cline says, are reason enough for people to seek help in reducing Internet use.

John Cline, "Sleep and the Internet Addict," *Sleepless in America* (blog), *Psychology Today,* September 11, 2011. www.psychologytoday.com.

was not tailored to Internet addicts, it was not helpful. He then attended a ten-week program in southern Utah that kept patients busy with outdoor activities, but he felt that without this distraction in the future, he would continue to have problems with gaming. As a result of reSTART, he says, "I don't think I'll go back to 'World of Warcraft' anytime soon."[81] To aid him and others in

A twenty-one-year-old gaming addict receives counseling at the Smith & Jones Centre in Amsterdam, Netherlands. The center, which specializes in gaming addiction, says its typical client is a male in his late teens who has dropped out of school and plays games for fifteen hours a day.

remaining free of their addictions, reSTART helps its graduating patients develop a recovery plan and keeps in contact with them about how to set limits on their personal use of the Internet or, if necessary, avoid it except for work-related tasks.

Different Approaches

Many of the addicts drawn to inpatient treatment centers are young people. For example, at the Smith & Jones Centre in Amsterdam, Netherlands, the first addiction treatment facility to specialize in gaming addictions, the typical client is a male in his late teens who has divorced parents, has dropped out of school, and who plays games for about fifteen hours a day. All of the addicts at the center are gamers because its founders believe patients will benefit from being around others with similar problems.

In contrast, the Illinois Institute for Addiction Recovery in

Peoria offers a six-week program of inpatient treatment to all kinds of addicts, who attend therapy groups together. A therapist for the program, Tonya Camacho, says that this approach is valid because all addicts deal with the same core issues. She explains, "The person who is addicted to his or her computer is going to have the same 'high' as the drug addict who is about to go see their drug dealer. Both are escapes from the real world." She adds that computer addicts have just as much trouble doing without their computers as drug addicts have doing without their drugs. "They just can't live without it,"[82] she says.

She reports that some people have abandoned the program because they could not handle being without Internet access. Others have smuggled devices like cell phones or tablets into the facility that would allow them to sneak onto the Internet. One of these people, a shopping addict, even went online while in treatment to order clothes that she then had shipped to the facility. "She had one of the worst online shopping addictions, but with in-patient therapy, she survived,"[83] says one institute staffer.

Indeed, there are those who would rather suffer from an Internet addiction than get help. For example, thirty-six-year-old Andrew Ross has shunned treatment in order to live in a tent near some railroad tracks and a highway in Oregon so he can focus on his desire to use the Internet. After getting up whenever he feels like it and using food stamps to buy something he can eat later, Andrew walks to Oregon State University to use a computer lab that is open to the public. Once there he spends ten or more hours on a computer, stopping only to eat his meal, perhaps after heating it in one of the university's microwave ovens.

Ross's addiction to the Internet involves multiple activities, including playing games like *World of Warcraft*, surfing the Internet, and reading online blogs and news sites. His younger brother Winston Ross, a journalist who has written about reSTART, reports, "He goes 'home' only when the lab closes. He's recently acquired a laptop, after much fundraising from sympathetic relatives, so he can now stay connected day and night, if he can find

"The person who is addicted to his or her computer is going to have the same 'high' as the drug addict who is about to go see their drug dealer. Both are escapes from the real world."[82]

— Therapist Tonya Camacho.

an open Wi-Fi hot spot."[84] Winston adds that his brother seems content with his life and might be using the Internet as a way to treat his diagnosed anxiety and depression, both of which did not respond to medical treatment. But Winston worries that the cold nights and other dangers of living out on the street will one day kill Andrew.

No Way to Treat?

Treatment for individuals as hooked on the Internet as Andrew Ross is, however, might not be possible given the ease of Internet access and the relative dearth of research and discussion to address the problem. Philip Tam, a psychiatrist and the president and co-founder of the Network for Internet Investigation and Research in Australia, says, "There is no simple, single way of 'controlling' or 'treating' 21st century problems such as internet addiction or video game addiction. Only a full, open and informed discussion by all stakeholders (parents, schools, opinion leaders, games & tech companies, teenagers) will have a lasting impact on this challenging problem."[85]

Tam believes more research on Internet addictions is needed because the Internet is such an important part of daily life and because such addictions are on the rise. He says:

> It is a cliché to state that computing, the Internet and gaming are now ubiquitous elements of daily life for most if not all people, particularly the young. The power and reach of the WWW [World Wide Web] most probably far exceeds any technology in humanity's short but eventful history. . . . In many ways, Internet Overuse/Addiction is the ultimate post-modern affliction for the 21st Century.[86]

Because the Internet is nearly impossible to avoid, most experts in the field agree that lifelong abstinence is not a viable treatment option for problematic Internet use. Instead, they say, moderation is the key, along with learning how to develop enough control to behave in healthy ways. But mental health professionals

"In many ways, Internet Overuse/Addiction is the ultimate post-modern affliction for the 21st Century."[86]

— Psychiatrist Philip Tam.

have yet to agree on just which treatment approach might be best for helping people reduce their Internet use to a level they can balance with other activities that include work and maintaining family relationships.

Facts

- Psychiatrist Jerald J. Block says that online addicts who try to quit cold turkey can become suicidal and/or aggressive toward others.

- A joint study by researchers from the United States and Israel published in 2010 indicates that behavioral addictions are best treated by a combination of therapy and medication for associated symptoms such as depression.

- China has more than three hundred treatment centers for online addictions.

- The treatment of compulsive gambling usually relies on more than one approach, including psychotherapy, medication, financial counseling, support groups, and self-help techniques.

- After leading a study in 2011 on online addictions among college students, Dimitri A. Christakis recommended that colleges develop awareness campaigns to educate students about online addictions and the options for treatment.

Source Notes

Introduction: Fun Activity or Uncontrollable Fixation?

1. Quoted in Jason Lee, "Former College Student Gets a Grip After Gaming Addiction," China Watch, April 13, 2013. www.thechinawatch.com.

2. Quoted in Lee, "Former College Student Gets a Grip After Gaming Addiction."

3. Quoted in Christopher S. Stewart, "Obsessed with the Internet: A Tale from China," *Wired*, January 13, 2010. www.wired.com.

4. John M. Grohol, "Why Internet Addiction Still Doesn't Exist," *World of Psychology* (blog), Psych Central, December 11, 2008. http://psychcentral.com.

5. John M. Grohol, "Internet Addiction Guide," Psych Central, October 26, 2012. http://psychcentral.com.

6. Ronald Pies, "Should DSM-V Designate 'Internet Addiction' a Mental Disorder?," *Psychiatry*, February 2009. www.ncbi.nlm.nih.gov.

7. Lisa Haisha, "Is Your Facebook Addiction a Sign of Loneliness?," *Huffington Post*, April 13, 2010. www.huffingtonpost.com.

Chapter One: What Are the Origins of Online Addiction Concerns?

8. Kimberly S. Young, "Internet Addiction over the Decade: A Personal Look Back," *World Psychiatry*, June 2010. www.ncbi.nlm.nih.gov.

9. Kimberly S. Young, "Internet Addiction: The Emergence of a New Clinical Disorder," *CyberPsychology & Behavior*, Fall 1998.

10. Kimberly S. Young, "Psychology of Computer Use: XL. Addictive Use of the Internet; a Case That Breaks the Stereotype," *Psychological Reports*, December 1996, p. 79.

11. Young, "Psychology of Computer Use," p. 79.

12. Young, "Internet Addiction."

13. NetAddiction, "Signs of Internet Addiction." www.netaddiction.com.

14. NetAddiction, "Internet Addiction Test." www.netaddiction .com.

15. Virginia Heffernan, "Miss G: A Case of Internet Addiction," *Opinionator* (blog), *New York Times*, April 9, 2011. http://opin ionator.blogs.nytimes.com.

16. Young, "Internet Addiction over the Decade."

17. E. Guy Coffee, "Internet-Addiction-Support-Group for Those with Acute or Chronic Internet Addiction Disorder," Heidelberg University, May 16, 1995. http://web.urz.uni-heidelberg .de.

18. Quoted in David Wallis, "Just Click No," *New Yorker*, January 13, 1997. www.newyorker.com.

19. Young, "Internet Addiction over the Decade."

20. Kimberly S. Young, *Caught in the Net.* New York: Wiley, 1998, p. 11.

21. Jerald J. Block, "Issues for DSM-V: Internet Addiction," *American Journal of Psychiatry*, March 1, 2008. http://ajp.psychiatry online.org.

22. Block, "Issues for DSM-V."

Chapter Two: Are Online Addictions Real Addictions?

23. Quoted in AFP Relaxnews, "Internet Withdrawal Symptoms Similar to 'Coming Off Illegal Drugs like Ecstasy,'" *New York Daily News*, February 28, 2013. www.nydailynews.com.

24. Alice G. Walton, "Internet Addiction Shows Up in the Brain," *Forbes*, January 17, 2012. www.forbes.com.

25. Quoted in Mara Tyler, "Social Media Addicts Get a Dopamine Rush When 'Using,'" Addiction Info, January 4, 2013. www .addictioninfo.org.

26. Vaughan Bell, "The Addiction Habit," *Slate*, December 18, 2009. www.slate.com.

27. Bell, "The Addiction Habit."

28. Quoted in Daniel Akst, "Interview with Gene M. Heyman: Is Addiction a Choice?," Boston.com, August 9, 2009. www.boston .com.

29. Quoted in Sarah Kershaw, "Hooked on the Web: Help Is on the Way," *New York Times*, December 1, 2005. www.nytimes.com.

30. Quoted in Matthew Sparkes, "Twitter and Facebook 'Addicts' Suffer Withdrawal Symptoms," *Telegraph* (London), April 11, 2013. www.telegraph.co.uk.

31. Quoted in Sparkes, "Twitter and Facebook 'Addicts' Suffer Withdrawal Symptoms."

32. Craig Nakken, *The Addictive Personality: Understanding the Addictive Process and Compulsive Behavior.* Center City, MN: Hazelden Foundation, 1996, p. 4.

33. Bell, "The Addiction Habit."

34. Todd Essig, "DSM-5 Opens the Diagnostic Door to 'Internet Addiction,'" *True/Slant* (blog), February 10, 2010. http://trueslant.com.

35. Heffernan, "Miss G."

36. Grohol, "Internet Addiction Guide."

Chapter Three: Are Addictions to Online Shopping and Social Networking Serious Problems?

37. Elizabeth M. Beck, "True Life: I Was a Preteen eBay Addict," *Dingus, Interrupted* (blog), March 5, 2013. http://elizabethmbeck.wordpress.com.

38. Beck, "True Life."

39. Beck, "True Life."

40. Quoted in CreditDonkey, "Survey: Online Shopping Addiction Statistics," February 13, 2013. www.creditdonkey.com.

41. Quoted in CreditDonkey, "Survey."

42. Quoted in Sara Cheshm Mishi and Manon Genevier, "The Reality of Shopping Addiction," *Corsair* (Santa Monica Community College), May 21, 2013. www.thecorsaironline.com.

43. Quoted in Daniel Bortz, "Confessions of Former Shopaholics," *U.S. News & World Report*, January 25, 2013. http://money.usnews.com.

44. Shulman Center for Compulsive Theft, Spending & Hoarding, "What Is Compulsive Shopping?" www.shopaholicsanonymous.org.

45. Quoted in Stanford School of Medicine, "Men, Women Have Similar Rates of Compulsive Buying, Stanford Study Shows," news release, September 30, 2006. http://med.stanford.edu.

46. Buzz Bissinger, "My Gucci Addiction," *GQ*, April 2013. www.gq.com.

47. Bissinger, "My Gucci Addiction."

48. Bissinger, "My Gucci Addiction."

49. Quoted in Mark Griffiths, "For Bidding, Plan It: Can Online Auctions (like E-Bay) Be Addictive?," *Drmarkgriffiths* (blog), June 27, 2012. http://drmarkgriffiths.wordpress.com.

50. Quoted in University of Bergen, "New Research About Facebook Addiction," July 5, 2012. www.uib.no.

51. University of Bergen, "New Research About Facebook Addiction."

52. Jeremy Dean, "Can You Be Addicted to Facebook or Is It Just a Bad Habit?," *PsyBlog*, January 14, 2013. www.spring.org.uk.

53. Diana Bocco and HowStuffWorks, "What Makes Networking Sites Addictive?," Curiosity, 2011. http://curiosity.discovery.com.

54. Laurel Snyder, "Addicted to Twitter," *Salon*, August 15, 2009. www.salon.com.

55. Snyder, "Addicted to Twitter."

56. Snyder, "Addicted to Twitter."

57. Quoted in Ruth Rettie, "An Exploration of Flow During Internet Use," *Internet Research*, May 1, 2001, p. 103.

58. Quoted in Timothy A. Pychyl, "Problematic Internet Use, Internet Procrastination and Flow," *Don't Delay* (blog), *Psychology Today*, March 23, 2009. www.psychologytoday.com.

59. Pychyl, "Problematic Internet Use, Internet Procrastination and Flow."

Chapter Four: Are Addictions to Gaming and Gambling Serious Problems?

60. Quoted in David Wright, "Game Theory: Are Video Games Addictive?," ABC World News, December 6, 2012. http://abcnews.go.com.

61. Quoted in Tim Martin, "*Farmville*: The Addiction," *News Blaze*, March 20, 2010. http://newsblaze.com.

62. Quoted in Martin, "*Farmville*."

63. Quoted in Martin, "*Farmville*."

64. Quoted in Wright, "Game Theory."

65. Quoted in Wright, "Game Theory."

66. Quoted in *USA Today*, "Video Games Can Have Harmful Effects for Addicts," March 1, 2013. www.usatoday.com.

67. Quoted in *USA Today*, "Video Games Can Have Harmful Effects for Addicts."

68. Quoted in Tamara Lush, "At War with *World of Warcraft*: An Addict Tells His Story," *Guardian* (Manchester, UK), August 29, 2011. www.guardian.co.uk.

69. Quoted in Lush, "At War with *World of Warcraft*."

70. Quoted in Lush, "At War with *World of Warcraft*."

71. Quoted in Lush, "At War with *World of Warcraft*."

72. Quoted in Mez Breeze, "A Quiet Killer: Why Video Games Are So Addictive," Next Web, January 12, 2013. http://thenextweb.com.

73. Grohol, "Internet Addiction Guide."

74. Josh Axelrad, "Online Gambling May Be Too Powerful for Regulation," *Guardian* (Manchester, UK), April 21, 2011. www.guardian.co.uk.

75. Axelrad, "Online Gambling May Be Too Powerful for Regulation."

76. *College and University Blog*, StateUniversity.com, "College Students and Internet Gambling," January 30, 2013. www.stateuniversity.com.

77. Quoted in Tracy McVeigh, "Britain's New Addicts: Women Who Gamble Online, at Home, and in Secret," *Guardian* (Manchester, UK), January 17, 2010. www.guardian.co.uk.

Chapter Five: How Can People Recover from Online Addictions?

78. Pauline, "My Story," Internet Addicts Anonymous, 2008. http://internetaddictsanonymous.pbworks.com.

79. Hunter R. Slaton, "Caught in the Web: An Internet Addict's Story," Fix, March 27, 2012. www.thefix.com.

80. Kate Abbott, "The Responsible Thief," Billfold, May 1, 2012. http://thebillfold.com.

81. Quoted in Nicholas K. Geranios, "Addicted to the Internet? There's Rehab for That," NBC News, September 3, 2009. www.nbcnews.com.

82. Quoted in Amy Jacobson and Emily Friedman, "Can't Stop Web Surfing? Go to Rehab," ABC News, August 7, 2008. http://abcnews.go.com.

83. Quoted in Jacobson and Friedman, "Can't Stop Web Surfing? Go to Rehab."

84. Winston Ross, "A World Wide Woe," Daily Beast, October 7, 2009. www.thedailybeast.com.

85. Quoted in Breeze, "A Quiet Killer: Why Video Games Are So Addictive."

86. Quoted in Breeze, "A Quiet Killer: Why Video Games Are So Addictive."

Related Organizations and Websites

American Gambling Association (AGA)
1299 Pennsylvania Ave. NW, Suite 1175
Washington, DC 20004
phone: (202) 552-2675
e-mail: info@americangaming.org
website: www.americangaming.org

Established in 1995 to represent the commercial casino entertainment industry, the AGA seeks to create a better understanding of gaming by providing the public, politicians, and the media information on gaming and gambling.

American Psychiatric Association (APA)
1000 Wilson Blvd., Suite 1825
Arlington, VA 22209
phone: (703) 907-7300; toll-free (888) 357-7924
e-mail: apa@psych.org
website: www.psych.org

Established in 1844, the APA is the world's largest psychiatric organization, representing more than thirty-three thousand psychiatric physicians worldwide. Its website provides information about mental health issues and APA publications, including all versions of the DSM.

Center for Internet Addiction
PO Box 72
Bradford, PA 16701
phone: (814) 451-2405
website: www.netaddiction.com

The Center for Internet Addiction offers counseling for problematic Internet use and related issues. Its website provides information on issues such as compulsive web surfing and online gambling and has a link to the *Recovery* blog.

Center for Internet and Technology Addiction

17 S. Highland St.
West Hartford, CT 06119
phone: (860) 561-8727
e-mail: drdave@virtual-addiction.com
website: www.virtual-addiction.com

The Center for Internet and Technology Addiction provides counseling, information, and resources related to online addictions. Its website offers articles, news releases, and videos related to these addictions.

Debtors Anonymous (DA)

General Service Office
PO Box 920888
Needham, MA 02492-0009
phone: (781) 453-2743
website: www.debtorsanonymous.org

Started in 1968 by a group of Alcoholics Anonymous members who were having trouble with overspending and gambling, DA seeks to help people understand their self-destructive behavior with money. Its website offers a wealth of information on the subject, including stories of recovery and help with getting support.

Gam-Anon

Gam-Anon International Service Office, Inc.
PO Box 157
Whitestone, NY 11357
phone: (718) 352-1671
website: www.gam-anon.org

Gam-Anon provides information to the public about compulsive gambling, with the aim of supporting not only compulsive gamblers but also their loved ones. Its website offers articles and fact sheets about issues related to compulsive gambling and helps people find twelve-step meetings to attend for support with a gambling problem.

Gamblers Anonymous (GA) International Service Office

PO Box 17173
Los Angeles, CA 90017
phone: (213) 386-8789
e-mail: isomain@gamblersanonymous.org
website: www.gamblersanonymous.org

Modeled after Alcoholics Anonymous, GA offers a twelve-step program for compulsive gamblers and support for their loved ones. Its website provides locations for fellowship meetings throughout the United States, as well as information about compulsive gambling.

Illinois Institute for Addiction Recovery

5409 N. Knoxville Ave.
Peoria, IL 61614
phone: (309) 691-1055; toll-free: (800) 522-3784
website: www.addictionrecov.org

The Illinois Institute for Addiction Recovery provides treatment for all forms of addiction, including Internet and gaming addictions. Its website offers information related to these issues and provides access to the institute's online magazine, *Paradigm*, which contains articles for professionals and individuals interested in addiction-related subjects.

Network for Internet Investigation and Research in Australia (NIIRA)

website: www.niira.org.au

The NIIRA offers online information about online addiction to both professionals and the general public and encourages research in the field of Internet addiction. Its founder, Philip Tam, is a leading expert on problematic Internet use.

On-Line Gamers Anonymous (OGA)

104 Miller Ln.
Harrisburg, PA 17110
phone: (612) 245-1115
e-mail: olga@olganon.org
website: www.olganon.org

The OGA is a fellowship group for compulsive gamers that also offers support for the loved ones of people suffering from a gaming addiction. Its website offers information about gaming addiction and online meetings of OGA support groups.

reSTART Internet and Technology Addiction Recovery

1001 290th Ave. SE
Fall City, WA 98024-7403
phone: (800) 682-6934
e-mail: contactus@netaddictionrecovery.com
website: www.netaddictionrecovery.com

reSTART is a Washington State inpatient treatment center for Internet addicts. The center's website offers information about online addiction and related problems.

Shopaholics Anonymous

Shulman Center
PO Box 250008
Franklin, MI 48025
phone: (248) 358-8508
website: www.shopaholicsanonymous.org

Part of the Shulman Center for Compulsive Theft, Spending & Hoarding, Shopaholics Anonymous provides counseling services and information to people suffering from compulsive shopping. Its website provides a test that people can take to determine whether their shopping behavior indicates an addiction.

Women Helping Women

e-mail: mslancelot@cox.net
website: www.femalegamblers.info

Created by addiction expert and former addict Marilyn Lancelot, author of the book *Gripped by Gambling*, the website Women Helping Women provides news and support for women gamblers in recovery.

Additional Reading

Books

Elias Aboujaoude, *Virtually You: The Dangerous Powers of the E-personality*. New York: Norton, 2011.

Nicholas Carr, *The Shallows: What the Internet Is Doing to Our Brains*. New York: Norton, 2011.

Holly Cefrey, *Frequently Asked Questions About Online Gaming Addiction*. New York: Rosen, 2010.

Mark Freeman, *Web Rehab: How to Give Up Your Internet Addiction Without Giving Up the Internet*. Toronto: Taketomi Media, 2011. Kindle edition.

Marilyn Lancelot, *Gripped by Gambling*. Tucson, AZ: Wheatmark, 2007.

Samuel C. McQuade, Sarah E. Gentry, and James P. Colt, *Internet Addiction and Online Gaming*. New York: Chelsea House, 2011.

Hannah O. Price, ed., *Internet Addiction*. Hauppauge, NY: Nova Science, 2011.

Kevin J. Roberts, *Cyber Junkie: Escape the Game and Internet Trap*. Center City, MN: Hazelden, 2010.

Ryan G. Van Cleave, *Unplugged: My Journey into the Dark World of Internet Game Addiction*. Deerfield Beach, FL: Health Communications, 2010.

Jean Riescher Westcott, *Video Game Addiction*. MyModernHealth FAQ. Dulles, VA: Mercury Learning and Information, 2013.

Kimberly S. Young and Cristiano Nabuco de Abreu, eds., *Internet Addiction: A Handbook and Guide to Evaluation and Treatment*. Hoboken, NJ: Wiley, 2011.

Internet Sources

Ryan Chang, "Internet Addiction Is a Real Thing. No, Really," *L Magazine*, September 3, 2013. www.thelmagazine.com/The Measure/archives/2013/09/03/internet-addiction-is-a-real -thing-no-really.

Taryn Davies, "Online Addiction Turning Us into Night Owls," *Female First*, September 2, 2013. www.femalefirst.co.uk/health /online-addiction-affecting-sleep-331895.html.

Petula Dvorak, "Online TV Addiction: Man, It's Hard to Shake," *Washington Post*, August 29, 2013. http://articles.washington post.com/2013-08-29/local/41572819_1_netflix-new-addic tion-new-drug.

Adina Kalish Neufeld, "The 12 Step E-Tox: How to Curb Your Electronic Device Addiction," *Huffington Post*, September 17, 2013. www.huffingtonpost.com/2013/09/17/12-step-e-tox-curb -electronic-device-addiction_n_3936807.html.

Victoria Woollaston, "Facebook Users Are Committing 'Virtual Identity Suicide' and Quitting the Site in Droves over Privacy and Addiction Fears," *Mail Online*, September 17, 2013. www .dailymail.co.uk/sciencetech/article-2423713/Facebook-users -committing-virtual-identity-suicide-quitting-site-droves -privacy-addiction-fears.html.

Leah Yamshon, "Nerd, Interrupted: Inside a Smartphone Addiction Treatment Center," *IT World*, September 17, 2013. www .itworld.com/370633/nerd-interrupted-inside-smartphone -addiction-treatment-center.

Index

Note: Boldface page numbers indicate illustrations.

Picture Credits

About the Author

Patricia D. Netzley is the author of more than fifty books for teens and adults. She also teaches writing and knitting and is a member of the Society of Children's Books Writers and Illustrators.